Building Resilience Field Manual

Praise for this book

'The Global WASH Cluster welcomes this handbook as a critical and timely resource that strengthens coordinated action across WASH, health, and nutrition actors in humanitarian crises. Its clear guidance and operational tool provides invaluable support for the humanitarian practitioners, government officials, and development partners to deliver more integrated, accountable, and resilience focused services to communities facing increasingly complex emergencies and humanitarian crises.'

Monica Ramos, Global WASH Cluster Coordinator, UNICEF

'This (is a) very comprehensive and informative document'

Margaret Montgomery, Technical officer, WHO

'The overall effort of drafting such a document is highly appreciated. It has significant information, in particular the various guidance tools e.g. on assessment, coordination, planning and strategy and implementation etc., which could be very useful for the stakeholders at the national, sub-national and local levels.'

Omar El Hattab, Chief Water, Environment and Sanitation, UNICEF

Building Resilience Field Manual

Coordination guidelines for integrated WASH, health, and nutrition programming in crisis settings

Nikolas Sorensen
Mariëlle Snel
James Ray III
Syed Yasir Ahmad Khan

Practical Action Publishing Ltd
25 Albert Street, Rugby,
Warwickshire, CV21 2SD, UK
www.practicalactionpublishing.com

A catalogue record for this book is available from the British Library & Library of Congress

ISBN 978-1-78853-472-7 Paperback
ISBN 978-1-78853-473-4 Digital book

Citation: Sorensen, N., Snel, M., Ray III, J., and Khan, S.Y.A. (2026) *Building Resilience Field Manual: Coordination Briefs for Integrated WASH, Health, and Nutrition Programming in Crisis Settings*, Rugby, UK: Practical Action Publishing https://doi.org/10.3362/9781788534734

Since 1974, Practical Action Publishing has published and disseminated books and information in support of international development work throughout the world. All print editions are produced and distributed via ethical and sustainable print on demand global facilities.

Practical Action Publishing is a trading name of Practical Action Publishing Ltd (Company Reg. No. 01159018 | VAT 880 9924 76). All profits are covenanted back to its parent group, Practical Action (Charity Reg. No. 247257).

Cover design by: Katarzyna Markowska, Practical Action Publishing
Typesetting by: vPrompt eServices, India

The manufacturer's authorised representative in the EU for product safety is Lightning Source France, 1 Av. Johannes Gutenberg, 78310 Maurepas, France. compliance@lightningsource.fr

Contents

Acknowledgements

We extend our sincere thanks to the incredible team at the WASH Road Map for making this work possible. We are also deeply grateful to the generous reviewers whose timely and thoughtful feedback significantly strengthened the final draft, including Bruce Gordon, Linda Doull, and Margaret Montgomery (WHO); Omar El Hattab, Sacha Greenberg, and Jamel Shah (UNICEF); Farah Al-Basha (IFRC); Jill John-Kall and Suzanne Brinkmann, with the International Medical Corps (IMC); and Nasr Mustafa with Save the Children International.

Additionally, we want to give special thanks to the International Medical Corps and Solidarités International for funding this field manual.

Executive summary

This comprehensive guide provides practical resources for integrating water, sanitation, and hygiene (WASH) interventions with health and nutrition actions during humanitarian emergencies. It offers a structured framework for coordinated, multisectoral response at both national and community levels faced by the compounding pressures of climate, conflict, and pandemic.

The guide addresses a critical need for greater coordination and integration in humanitarian contexts. It serves as an actionable resource that prioritizes government leadership at all levels, supporting national and local government officials, ministry staff, and public sector institutions alongside international, regional, and community WASH, health, and nutrition professionals. The guidelines specifically emphasize strengthening government systems and capacities as the foundation for sustainable emergency response.

Components and structure

This guide comprises five interconnected components built around the four coordination briefs (briefs 1–4):

- Integration by design: Coordination guidelines for resilient WASH programming in humanitarian contexts (simplified introduction)
- Brief 1. Integration in emergencies: Guideline for coordinating WASH with health at the national level
- Brief 2. Integration in emergencies: Guideline for coordinating WASH with nutrition at the national level
- Brief 3. Integration in emergencies: Guideline for coordinating WASH with health at the community level
- Brief 4. Integration in emergencies: Guideline for coordinating WASH with nutrition at the community level

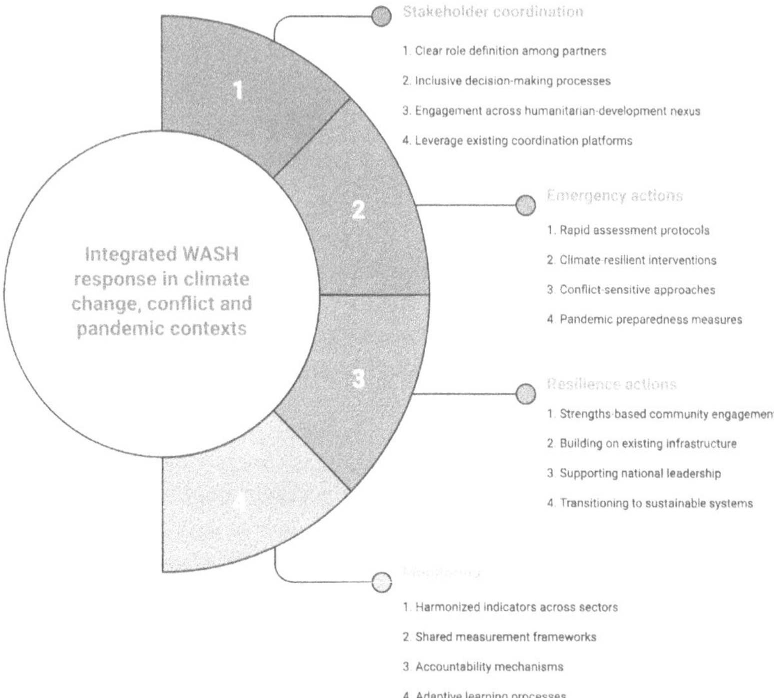

Figure 1 These interconnected domains provide a comprehensive framework for designing, implementing, and evaluating integrated WASH responses.

The content is structured around four interdependent domains, as illustrated in Figure 1:

- stakeholder coordination
- emergency WASH actions
- resilience actions
- monitoring and evaluation.

Each section combines strategic framing with operational tools to guide the assessment, planning, and implementation of WASH interventions responsive to complex crisis dynamics. Annex 2 outlines the eight foundational principles that guide decision-making across all four coordination guidelines.

This practitioner-oriented guide provides concrete protocols and tools to bridge WASH, health, and nutrition interventions. It equips decision-makers and implementers to:

- assess multi-dimensional risks and plan joint interventions
- optimize synergies between health, nutrition, and WASH programmes
- align short-term emergency activities with long-term development goals
- engage communities as central drivers of the response
- adapt global standards to local realities and capacities
- strengthen accountability for holistic, sustainable, people-centred impacts.

The guidelines focus specifically on the national and community levels, recognizing that these are the key entry points for fostering local ownership, strengthening existing systems, and ensuring the relevance and sustainability of interventions.

This document is important for anyone involved in humanitarian WASH, health, or nutrition programming, as it provides a roadmap for delivering integrated, localized services in the face of increasing operational constraints. The guidelines are designed to be practical and modular, allowing practitioners to quickly access the specific guidance and tools they need.

The primary audience for this document includes WASH, health, and nutrition programme managers, coordinators, and advisers across humanitarian and development organizations, as well as national and local government officials responsible for emergency preparedness and response. Field-level practitioners, such as public health officers, community mobilizers, and frontline service providers, will also benefit from the concrete guidance and tools for operationalizing integrated approaches.

Audience and application

This guide is intended for a wide range of humanitarian practitioners engaged in WASH, health, and nutrition preparedness and response, including:

- government officials in relevant line ministries
- WASH, health, and nutrition cluster/sector coordinators

- UN agency emergency focal points
- non-governmental organization (NGO) programme managers and technical advisers
- frontline service providers in health, nutrition, and WASH
- community-based organizations and volunteer networks.

The coordination guidelines in the briefs provide a flexible roadmap that can be applied across the humanitarian programme cycle through:

- *preparedness*: adapt the tools and coordination mechanisms to emergency-prone contexts as part of contingency planning and capacity building
- *response*: follow the guidelines to rapidly activate and sustain coordinated WASH services from the acute emergency phase through to early recovery
- *recovery*: continue applying the guidance to facilitate a smooth transition to sustainable, locally managed WASH and health-nutrition systems.

Adaptability

While grounded in global evidence and standards, the coordination guidelines are designed to adapt to diverse country contexts and emergency situations. The guidance can be tailored to align with existing policies, capacities, and cultural norms at national and subnational levels. To support implementation, the full text includes a Practitioners' Toolkit with detailed tools and templates. Annex 1 of this guide provides a 'quick start guide' linking each section to corresponding toolkit resources.

INTRODUCTION

Integration by design

Coordination guidelines for resilient WASH programming in humanitarian contexts

Introduction

The global humanitarian landscape is increasingly characterized by protracted crises, each defined by greater complexity and scope (Guinote, 2018; Sorensen and Snel, 2022; Snel et al., 2024). The combined pressures of climate change, conflict, and pandemics (CCP) are straining humanitarian systems by intensifying water scarcity, triggering displacement, undermining essential services, and exposing critical weaknesses in fragile settings. The growing impact of these interconnected challenges requires reevaluating how WASH services are designed and delivered. This guide introduces the WASH Road Map's new coordination guidelines with the aim of integrating the coordination of the humanitarian and development WASH sectors with those of health and nutrition and streamlining community and national decision-making.

The global humanitarian and development landscape is facing an unprecedented funding crisis. As international donors increasingly concentrate their limited resources on immediate humanitarian crises, the space for long-term development programming continues to shrink, creating a critical gap that must be filled by other actors and approaches. This dramatic shift in humanitarian and development financing necessitates a fundamental reorientation toward government-led response mechanisms and domestic resource mobilization. As international actors shift their focus to prioritize acute humanitarian interventions, national governments must assume a greater responsibility for both emergency preparedness and long-term development. These guidelines provide concrete pathways for this transition by:

- strengthening government coordination capacity at the national and local levels to manage both emergencies and development programming
- building technical expertise within relevant ministries and departments to reduce dependence on international technical assistance
- developing sustainable financing mechanisms through government budgets and domestic resource mobilization
- supporting governments to design development programmes that inherently strengthen emergency preparedness and resilience.

Evolving humanitarian architecture and cluster integration

Parallel to shifts in the funding landscape, the humanitarian coordination architecture is facing increasing pressure to adapt. Integrated cluster approaches showcase the critical value of coordinated programming in enhancing WASH, health, and nutrition outcomes while maximizing impact on affected communities.

Potential benefits of cluster integration:

- Unified assessment and analysis frameworks that capture WASH–health–nutrition interconnections.
- Streamlined coordination, reducing the burden on government and partner participation.
- Joint resource mobilization that addresses multisectoral needs through unified proposals.
- Integrated information management systems, avoiding duplication and data gaps.
- Harmonized standards and indicators facilitating cross-sectoral programming.
- Reduced competition between sectors for limited resources.

Challenges and trade-offs:

- Risk of losing technical depth and specialized expertise within each sector.
- Potential marginalization of sectors perceived as less 'life-saving' in acute emergencies.

- Complexity of managing diverse technical competencies within unified structures.
- Challenges in maintaining accountability for sector-specific standards and outcomes.

These guidelines are designed to provide a comprehensive guide for WASH practitioners during the critical first 90 days of an emergency response. Each guideline is organized around four key domains: stakeholder coordination, emergency WASH actions, resilience actions, and monitoring and evaluation. They offer step-by-step guidance, real-world examples, and adaptable tools specifically for emergency response coordination and implementation during this crucial initial period.

Understanding CCP pressures

CCP represent three compounding pressures that fundamentally reshape how WASH practitioners must design and deliver services in humanitarian contexts. This lens acknowledges the distinct and overlapping challenges that climate change, violent conflict, and disease outbreaks present for WASH services and the communities that rely on them. By centring community resilience and agency, the guidelines presented here offer practical pathways for local and national actors to coordinate integrated WASH responses that address immediate needs while building sustainable systems capable of withstanding future shocks. These guidelines are also grounded in the CCP lens. When applied to these guidelines, a strengths-based lens shifts implementation from a model of substitution to one of empowerment, creating space for national and community actors to lead sustainable, long-term WASH interventions, especially in protracted and complex crisis settings.

The triple nexus (or humanitarian–development–peace nexus) has been identified as a critical means of addressing the growing number of protracted crises worldwide (Sorensen and Snel, 2022; Snel and Sorensen, 2023). The recent creation of the Joint Operational Framework has helped clarify the importance of the triple nexus and highlighted key coordination pathways to help ensure its successful implementation (Grieve, 2023; Grieve et al., 2023). The argument presented here emphasizes that CCP represent the most significant challenges to integrating WASH across the humanitarian–development nexus. Each guideline has been developed to help suggest and establish standard measurements and indicators across the humanitarian–development nexus during the onset, transition, and recovery stages of a crisis. The guidelines also aim to enhance intersectoral coordination, support affected populations, and prioritize locally led and sustainable interventions (Dickin et al., 2022; Heylen et al., 2022; Srivastava et al., 2022; Huang et al., 2023; Yasmin et al., 2023; Abbara et al., 2024).

CCP place unique pressures on WASH services that require specific programmatic responses. We emphasize here that solutions must address immediate needs while building resilience to future crises. The impact of these three pressures is well documented and thoroughly discussed. Climate change displaces populations and stresses urban systems, necessitating localized, context-specific WASH interventions (Baxter et al., 2022; Dickin et al., 2022; Kim et al., 2022; Srivastava et al., 2022; ACF, 2023; Huang et al., 2023; Yasmin et al., 2023; Abbara et al., 2024; Mansour, 2024; Snel et al., 2024). Conflict limits access to resources, as seen in areas such as Gaza, Yemen, or Myanmar, necessitating conflict-sensitive programming and local leadership (Al-Awlaqi et al., 2022; Kim et al., 2022; Maryati and Azizah, 2022). The COVID-19 pandemic exposed gaps in infrastructure and coordination, underscoring the need for adaptable institutional responses to mitigate future crises while maintaining essential services (Heylen et al., 2022; Kim et al., 2022; Maryati and Azizah, 2022).

While these crises present considerable challenges, they also offer a critical opportunity to rethink WASH implementation systems by strategically integrating service delivery with other sectors. Evidence demonstrates that linking WASH with health, nutrition, shelter, education, and child protection can significantly amplify outcomes for affected populations. The connections between WASH services and health outcomes, particularly in humanitarian contexts, are well established (Sorensen and Snel, 2023; Zinszer and Abuzerr, 2024). Nutrition-sensitive WASH programmes have proven highly effective in reducing childhood stunting and malnutrition in vulnerable communities (Dodos and Riems, 2023; Yasmin et al., 2023). WASH integration with shelter and food systems enhances resilience in refugee contexts (Srivastava et al., 2022; Webb, 2023). Meanwhile, school-based initiatives foster long-term hygiene behaviours and have been shown to boost school attendance, particularly among girls (Corwith and Sorensen, 2023; Mansour, 2024). Finally, incorporating WASH into the design and placement of shelters, camps, and community spaces is essential to child protection efforts, particularly for women, girls, and people living with disabilities, and is closely linked to long-term safety, education, and health outcomes (Srivastava et al., 2022; Jeffery, 2023).

These guidelines operationalize multisectoral approaches by providing a clear framework for integrated action across CCP contexts. Focusing on the integration of WASH with health and nutrition, they are organized around four key domains: stakeholder coordination, emergency WASH actions, resilience actions, and monitoring and evaluation. Each section combines strategic framing with operational tools, offering step-by-step guidance for assessment, planning, implementation, and evaluation.

Enablers for intersectoral coordination

Multisectoral champions play a crucial role in fostering collaboration and ensuring alignment among diverse stakeholders. Leaders who support intersectoral coordination (ISC) initiatives help close the gaps between sectors and drive collective action. Broader findings also underscore the importance of accountability mechanisms and leadership in aligning stakeholder priorities for integrated WASH programming (Dickin et al., 2022). These enablers highlight the importance of strategic action and innovative thinking in overcoming barriers to ISC. By leveraging existing infrastructure, empowering communities, and fostering cross-sectoral leadership, ISC can serve as a powerful tool for addressing the complex challenges present in CCP contexts.

Community engagement is a critical driver of ISC success, with localization serving as the cornerstone principle for effective humanitarian response. Localization – the meaningful transfer of decision-making power, resources, and implementation to local actors – is essential as international funding diminishes. Local actors play a pivotal role in designing and executing context-specific solutions that reflect the needs and realities of affected populations.

Key enablers for enhancing ISC effectiveness in addressing CCP challenges include leveraging existing infrastructure to reduce costs and streamline programme scalability, such as the Clean Clinic Approach in healthcare facilities (Lopez et al., 2020), and climate-resilient, community-led WASH strategies in schools (Mansour 2024). Building trust with donors and introducing resilience activities into emergency programming through evidence-based decision-making are other crucial factors. Training WASH staff, fieldworkers, and volunteers to connect WASH with other priorities for effective knowledge management and integration, and transitioning from short-term responses to development-focused, holistic approaches by securing local, regional, and national buy-in (Huang et al., 2023) are also key enablers.

Practical implementation of these enablers requires specific tools and frameworks. For harmonizing metrics across sectors, established frameworks such as the WHO/UNICEF Joint Monitoring Programme (JMP), WASH FIT (water and sanitation for health facility improvement tool), and the Sustainable Sanitation Alliance's (SuSanA) M&E (monitoring and evaluation) toolkit provide tested approaches (see the detailed discussion in the following section, 'Measurement and indicators'). Similarly, innovative financing mechanisms, including pooled funds and blended finance arrangements, are emerging to address the challenge of siloed funding, though implementation remains an evolving area of practice.

Measurement and indicators

Effective measurement and indicators are critical for evaluating and improving ISC to address CCP. Harmonized and practical evaluation frameworks ensure accountability, facilitate learning, and guide sustainable improvements. Alignment of indicators presents a central challenge in the evaluation of ISC. Harmonizing metrics across sectors is crucial for capturing nuanced impacts. For example, the Global Trachoma Mapping Project highlights the challenges in aligning data collection scales across the WASH and health sectors. Misaligned metrics can create gaps in monitoring and hinder evidence-based decision-making (Dickin et al., 2022; Gooding et al., 2022; Chandratreya, 2023; D'Mello-Guyett et al., 2024). Developing shared measurement frameworks can ensure that ISC outcomes are tracked and evaluated more accurately.

Joint measurement frameworks for integrated programming

Effective integrated WASH programming requires standardized measurement tools that capture cross-sectoral outcomes. Several established frameworks can facilitate this integration:

- *WHO/UNICEF JMP*: this provides standardized WASH indicators that can be integrated with health and nutrition monitoring systems. The JMP framework enables the tracking of safely managed water and sanitation services, with indicators directly linkable to health outcomes, such as reductions in diarrheal disease and improvements in nutritional status (WHO and UNICEF, n.d.a, n.d.b).
- *WASH FIT*: this offers a practical approach for measuring and improving WASH conditions in healthcare facilities. This tool integrates quality improvement methodologies with WASH standards, creating measurable links between infrastructure improvements and health service delivery outcomes (WHO and UNICEF, 2022).
- *SuSanA's M&E toolkit*: this provides comprehensive M&E resources that span the humanitarian–development continuum. The toolkit includes indicators for sustainability, functionality, and cross-sectoral impacts, enabling programmes to track both immediate outputs and long-term systems strengthening (Okoth, 2018).
- *Integrated Phase Classification (IPC) for WASH*: when combined with IPC for food security and nutrition, this framework enables unified severity analysis across sectors, supporting prioritization and resource allocation decisions (IPC, n.d.).

These frameworks should be adapted to local contexts while maintaining core standardized indicators that enable comparison and aggregation across programmes and regions.

The guidelines provide harmonized metrics to track outcomes across sectors. They recommend using geospatial tools to reveal gaps in WASH coverage and identify disease hot spots for targeted health investments. Composite indices assess community resilience in WASH, health, and nutrition. A key aspect is linking thorough monitoring with inclusive decision-making, ensuring that affected communities have a voice in interventions, and promoting accountability and local ownership. Implementing these systems is vital for practical evaluation and underscores the necessity of shared responsibility among sectors. Ultimately, these guidelines aim to catalyse a shift toward a more localized and integrated approach to WASH programming in complex crises.

With the downsizing of the UN system, the onus is increasingly on international and national actors to proactively seek out and share data to enable an effective humanitarian response. It is critical that all humanitarian actors, particularly local responders who are often closest to the crisis, prioritize the timely collection and sharing of their data through such collaborative mechanisms. Establishing clear data sharing protocols and capacities before a crisis hits can enable a more agile, transparent, and coordinated response when it matters most.

Conclusion

Recent announcements of significant reductions in international humanitarian assistance present both substantial challenges and potential opportunities (Sabow et al., 2025). National governments and local groups must take a larger role in crisis response and building resilience. These guidelines are vital in strengthening their capacities and promoting local solutions. Effective coordination and integration across sectors will be crucial to responding efficiently to crises and building resilience for the future in this new, resource-constrained environment. By focusing on coordination, integration, and resource efficiency, the WASH sector can adapt to this new reality and effectively address the needs of affected communities (see Figure 2).

These guidelines are essential tools, not silver bullet solutions. The conceptual framework and evidence base presented in this section provide the foundation for the four coordination guidelines that follow. Briefs 1–4 in the following sections translate the understanding of CCP pressures, barriers analysis, and enablers into actionable guidance organized around four core domains: stakeholder coordination, emergency WASH actions, resilience actions, and monitoring and evaluation. Each guideline addresses specific coordination challenges at the national and community levels while maintaining a focus on integrating WASH with health and nutrition outcomes. We acknowledge that there is some overlap among the guidelines, which was considered unavoidable due to

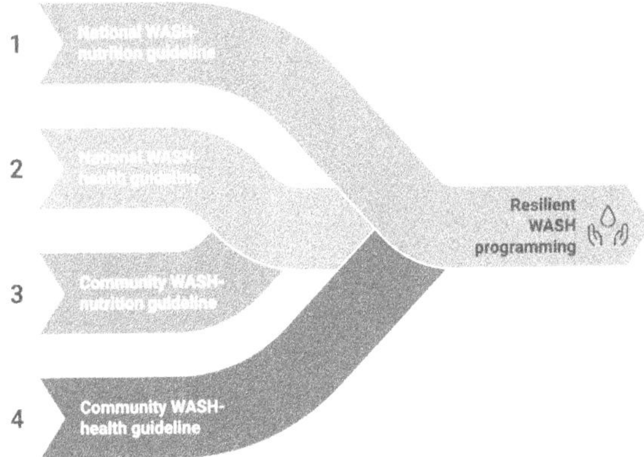

Figure 2 Guidelines for integrated WASH with health and nutrition.

the interconnectedness of integrated programming. As practitioners frequently operate within specific sectors or levels, we decided to develop four distinct guidelines to facilitate access and enable each guideline to serve as an individual resource when needed. Although we cannot foresee every practitioner's requirement, our goal was to provide sufficient and valuable starting points so that decision-makers would not have to start from scratch in a new emergency response. Together, these components provide a comprehensive roadmap for transitioning from a theoretical understanding of integrated WASH programming to its practical implementation in complex humanitarian contexts.

Bibliography

Abbara, Aula, Reem Abu Shomar, Marwa Daoudy, Ghassan Abu Sittah, Muhammad H. Zaman, and Mark Zeitoun. 2024. 'Water, Health, and Peace: A Call for Interdisciplinary Research'. *The Lancet* 403 (10435): 1427–29. https://doi.org/10.1016/S0140-6736(24)00588-9

Action Against Hunger (ACF). 2023. 'World's Water Funding Crisis: How Donors Are Missing the Mark'. ACF. https://www.actionagainsthunger.org/publications/2023-water-funding-gap-report/

Al-Awlaqi, Sameh, Fekri Dureab, and Marzena Tambor. 2022. 'The National Health Cluster in Yemen: Assessing the Coordination of Health Response during Humanitarian Crises'. *Journal of*

International Humanitarian Action 7 (1): 9. https://doi.org/10.1186/s41018-022-00117-y

Baxter, Louisa, Catherine R. McGowan, Sandra Smiley, Liliana Palacios, Carol Devine, and Cristian Casademont. 2022. 'The Relationship between Climate Change, Health, and the Humanitarian Response'. *The Lancet* 400 (10363): 1561–63. https://doi.org/10.1016/S0140-6736(22)01991-2

Chandratreya, Abhijit. 2023. 'Financing Strategies for Water, Sanitation, and Hygiene (WASH) Initiatives: A Comprehensive Review'. *Community Practitioner* 20 (10).

Corwith, Anne, and Erin Sorensen. 2023. 'Integrated WASH and Education'. In *Addressing Conflict, COVID-19, and Climate Change: A Multisectoral Approach to Integrated WASH Programming*, 135–152, edited by Mariëlle Snel and Nikolas Sorensen. Rugby UK: Practical Action Publishing Ltd.

Dickin, Sarah, Abu Syed, Nishrin Qowamuna, George Njoroge, Carla Liera, Mohamad Mova Al'Afghani, Sidratun Chowdhury, Zoraida Sanchez, Abdulwahab Moalin Salad, Keren Winferford, Erma Uijtewaal, Virginia Roaf, John Butterworth, and Juliet Willett. 2022. 'Assessing Mutual Accountability to Strengthen National WASH Systems and Achieve the SDG Targets for Water and Sanitation'. *H2Open Journal* 5 (2): 166–79. https://doi.org/10.2166/h2oj.2022.032

D'Mello-Guyett, Lauren, Camille Heylen, Elsa Rohm, Jane Falconer, Jean Lapegue, Robert Dreibelbis, Monica Ramos, Oliver Cumming, and Daniele Lantagne. 2024. 'Research Priorities for Water, Sanitation and Hygiene (WASH) in Humanitarian Crises: A Global Prioritisation Exercise'. *PLOS Water* 3 (3): e0000217. https://doi.org/10.1371/journal.pwat.0000217

Dodos, Jovana, and Bram Riems. 2023. 'WASH-Nutrition Integration: For Vulnerable Populations Affected by Conflict, Climate Change and the COVID-19 Pandemic'. In *Addressing Conflict, COVID-19, and Climate Change: A Multisectoral Approach to Integrated WASH Programming*, edited by Mariëlle Snel and Nikolas Sorensen, 1–32. Rugby UK: Practical Action Publishing.

Gooding, Kate, Maria Paola Bertone, Giulia Loffreda, and Guidelinhie Witter. 2022. 'How Can We Strengthen Partnership and Coordination for Health System Emergency Preparedness and Response? Findings from a Synthesis of Experience across Countries Facing Shocks'. *BMC Health Services Research* 22 (1): 1441. https://doi.org/10.1186/s12913-022-08859-6

Grieve, Timothy. 2023. 'A WASH Framework to Address Conflict, COVID-19, and Climate Change: Leveraging the Humanitarian–Development–Peace Nexus'. In *Addressing Conflict, COVID-19, and Climate Change: A Multisectoral Approach to Integrated WASH Programming,* edited by Mariëlle Snel and Nikolas Sorensen, 33–65. Rugby UK: Practical Action Publishing Ltd.

Grieve, Timothy, Thilo Panzerbieter, and Johannes Rück. 2023. *WASH Resilience, Conflict Sensitivity and Peacebuilding: Joint Operational Framework*. Triple Nexus in WASH Initiative. https://www.wash-net.de/en/triple-nexus-wash/joint-operational-framework/

Guinote, Filipa Schmitz. 2018. 'A Humanitarian-Development Nexus That Works – World'. ReliefWeb. June 21. https://reliefweb.int/report/world/humanitarian-development-nexus-works

Heylen, Camille, Travis Yates, Langley Topper, Franck Bouvet, Dominique Porteaud, Monica Ramos, Jean McCluskey, and Daniele Lantagne. 2022. 'Realtime Assessment of WASH Coordination in Three Humanitarian Emergencies'. *PLOS Water* 1 (11): e0000047. https://doi.org/10.1371/journal.pwat.0000047

Huang, Ai-Ju, David Githiri Njoroge, Lilian Otiego, and Alexander Danilenko. 2023. 'From a Humanitarian to Development Approach: Uganda's Ground-Breaking Journey to Achieve Sustainable Provision of Water Services to Refugees and Host Communities'. The World Bank.

IPC. n.d. 'IPC Overview and Classification System'. IPC – Integrated Food Security Phase Classification. https://www.ipcinfo.org/ipcinfo-website/ipc-overview-and-classification-system/en/

Jeffery, Allison. 2023. 'Child Protection and WASH Integration'. In *Addressing Conflict, COVID-19, and Climate Change: A Multisectoral Approach to Integrated WASH Programming,* edited by Mariëlle Snel and Nikolas Sorensen, 1–32. Rugby UK: Practical Action Publishing.

Kim, Junghwan, Erica Hagen, Zacharia Muindi, Gaston Mbonglou, and Melinda Laituri. 2022. 'An Examination of Water, Sanitation, and Hygiene (WASH) Accessibility and Opportunity in Urban Informal Settlements during the COVID-19 Pandemic: Evidence from Nairobi, Kenya'. *Science of The Total Environment* 823 (June): 153398. https://doi.org/10.1016/j.scitotenv.2022.153398

Lopez, Jason, Sergio Tumax Sierra, Ana María Rodas Cardona, and Stephen Sara. 2020. 'Implementing the Clean Clinic Approach Improves Water, Sanitation, and Hygiene Quality in Health Facilities in the Western Highlands of Guatemala'. *Global Health: Science and Practice* 8 (2): 256–69. https://doi.org/10.9745/GHSP-D-19-00413

Mansour, Luna. 2024. 'Water, Sanitation, and Hygiene in Schools: A Global Analysis of Bottlenecks and Climate Resilient Strategies'. TRITA-ABE-MBT. Master's Thesis, KTH, Sustainable Development, Environmental Science and Engineering.

Maryati, Sri, and Devi Martina Azizah. 2022. 'Innovation During COVID-19 Pandemic: Water, Sanitation, and Hygiene in Informal

Settlements'. *Pertanika Journal of Social Sciences and Humanities.* https://api.semanticscholar.org/CorpusID:249739197

Okoth, Simon. 2018. 'SuSanA Monitoring and Evaluation Framework: Towards Sustainable Sanitation for All'. Sustainable Sanitation Alliance (SuSanA).

Sabow, Adam, Matt Craven, Matt Wilson, Michael Conway, Tina Holt, Connor Rochford, and Sarah Anderson. 2025. 'The Future of Foreign Aid: A Generational Shift'. McKinsey & Company. https://www.mckinsey.com/industries/social-sector/our-insights/a-generational-shift-the-future-of-foreign-aid#/

Snel, Mariëlle, and Nikolas Sorensen, eds. 2023. *Addressing Conflict, COVID-19, and Climate Change: A Multisectoral Approach to Integrated WASH Programming*. Rugby UK: Practical Action Publishing Ltd.

Snel, Mariëlle, Nikolas Sorensen, and Reed Power. 2024. *Climate Change and Water Scarcity in the Middle East: A Transitional Approach*, 1st edn. London: Routledge. https://doi.org/10.4324/9781003436706

Sorensen, Nikolas, and Mariëlle Snel. 2022. 'The New Reality: Perspectives on Future Integrated WASH'. *Waterlines* 41 (1): 65–80. https://doi.org/10.3362/1756-3488.20-00007OA

———. 2023. 'Integrating WASH with Health in Humanitarian Settings'. In *Addressing Conflict, COVID-19, and Climate Change: A Multisectoral Approach to Integrated WASH Programming*, 67–84, edited by Marielle Snel and Nikolas Sorensen. Rugby UK: Practical Action Publishing Ltd.

Srivastava, Shilpi, Jeremy Allouche, Roz Price, and Tina Nelis. 2022. 'Bringing WASH into the Water–Energy–Food Nexus in Humanitarian Settings'. *IDS Working Paper 563*, Brighton: Institute of Development Studies. https://doi.org/DOI:10.19088/IDS.2022.006

Webb, Susannah. 2023. 'Integrated WASH and Shelter'. In *Addressing Conflict, COVID-19, and Climate Change: A Multisectoral Approach to Integrated WASH Programming*, edited by Mariëlle Snel and Nikolas Sorensen, 1–32. Rugby UK: Practical Action Publishing.

WHO and UNICEF. 2022. *Water and Sanitation for Health Facility Improvement Tool (WASH FIT): A Practical Guide for Improving Quality of Care through Water, Sanitation and Hygiene in Health Care Facilities*. 2nd edn. Geneva: World Health Organization (WHO).

WHO and UNICEF. n.d.a. 'About the JMP'. https://washdata.org/how-we-work/about-jmp

WHO and UNICEF. n.d.b. 'WHO/UNICEF Joint Monitoring Programme'. https://washdata.org/

Yasmin, T., S. Dhesi, I. Kuznetsova, R. Cooper, S. Krause, and I. Lynch. 2023. 'A System Approach to Water, Sanitation, and Hygiene Resilience and Sustainability in Refugee Communities'. *International Journal of Water Resources Development* 39 (5): 691–723. https://doi.org/10.1080/07900627.2022.2131362

Zinszer, Kate, and Samer Abuzerr. 2024. 'Water, Sanitation, and Hygiene Insecurity and Infectious Disease Outbreaks among Internally Displaced Populations in Gaza: Implications of Conflict-Driven Displacement on Public Health'. *Journal of Water, Sanitation and Hygiene for Development* 14 (11): 1182–92. https://doi.org/10.2166/washdev.2024.361

CHAPTER 1

Brief 1. Integration in emergencies

Guideline for coordinating WASH with health at the national level

Source document: Chapter 2 in Sorensen, Nikolas, Mariëlle Snel, James Ray III, and Syed Yasir Ahmad Khan. 2026. *Building Resilience: Coordination Guidelines for Integrated WASH, Health, and Nutrition Programming in Crisis Settings*. Practical Action Publishing. http://doi.org/10.3362/9781788534710

1.1 Executive summary

This guideline provides essential coordination guidance for national officials overseeing WASH initiatives and health initiatives, respectively, during emergencies. It supports rapid response while emphasizing long-term resilience, serving as one of four complementary guidelines designed as an integrated framework for WASH coordination with health and nutrition at both national and community levels. This guideline was developed by the WASH Road Map in consultation with numerous other professionals.

1.1.1 Purpose

This guideline helps national-level officials and humanitarian coordinators integrate WASH and health interventions during emergencies through structured, time-bound actions. It upholds the rights outlined in the Humanitarian Charter and aligns with global commitments to advance universal health coverage and primary healthcare.

1.1.2 Key actions

Actions	*WASH*	*Health*	*Timeframe*	*Guideline sections*	*Practitioners' Toolkit sections*
Activate coordination platform and establish roles	Establish co-leadership with government and WHO; identify WASH representatives and define roles	Establish co-leadership with government and UNICEF; identify health representatives and define roles	Within 48 hours	1.2.4, 1.2.8, 1.2.9, 1.2.10	1.1, 1.2, 1.5, 1.6, 1.7
Conduct rapid integrated assessments	Lead comprehensive WASH needs, capacity, and stakeholder assessment	Lead assessments of WASH in health facilities and map health stakeholders	Days 1–14	1.2.9, 1.3.1.1	1.3, 2.1, 2.2, 2.3, 2.4, 2.6, 3.4, 3.5
Provide emergency WASH services	Provide minimum WASH services as per minimum standards; distribute supplies; ensure WASH in health facilities meets minimum standards	Health facility managers monitor WASH infrastructure and alert appropriate staff of needs	Days 1–14	1.3.1.2, 1.3.1.3, 1.3.1.4, 1.3.1.6	2.4, 2.5, 4.4, 4.5
Establish integrated monitoring and feedback	Adapt and utilize existing joint indicators and develop community feedback systems to the local context	Adapt and utilize existing indicators and community feedback mechanisms	By day 30	1.2.9, 1.2.11, 1.3.2.5, 1.4	5.1, 5.3, 5.4, 5.6, 3.3

(Continues)

(Continued)

Actions	*WASH*	*Health*	*Timeframe*	*Guideline sections*	*Practitioners' Toolkit sections*
Implement cross-sectoral coordination	Engage in joint planning with health sector; coordinate hygiene promotion	Coordinate with WASH counterparts to integrate WASH interventions with health interventions	Days 14–45	1.2.10, 1.3.1.6	3.1, 3.6, 3.7, 4.1, 4.2, 4.7
Address specialized needs	Control vector transmission when relevant; support outbreak response	Implement activities for vector-borne disease prevention, treatment, and control including health education, disease surveillance and utilizing national treatment protocols	Days 14–90	1.3.1.5, 1.3.1.6	2.3, 4.4, 5.2
Strengthen local capacity and transition planning	Build community and partner capacity; support transition to local management	Lead health system WASH capacity and sustainability planning	Days 30–90	1.3.2.1, 1.3.2.2, 1.3.2.3, 1.3.2.4	3.4, 3.6, 4.2, 4.8, 4.9
Review policies and document learning	Review WASH policies; capture and share lessons learned	Review health policies; document health facility improvements	Throughout response	1.2.8, 1.3.1.7, 1.3.2.6	1.3, 5.5, 4.3, 4.6, 4.10

1.1.3 Framework pillars

Five pillars structure this guideline:

1. *National coordination*: Establishing inclusive mechanisms across ministries, agencies, and partners.
2. *Strategic assessment*: Identifying WASH and health strengths, needs, risks, and capacities.
3. *Integrated service delivery*: Addressing immediate needs while strengthening local systems.
4. *National capacity building*: Developing sustainable crisis preparedness and response capabilities.
5. *National monitoring*: Tracking performance to ensure accountability and inform future strategies.

Throughout, this guideline mainstreams climate resilience, protection, gender equity, and social inclusion while defining clear roles across government, humanitarian organizations, and community partners.

1.2 Stakeholder coordination

The integration of WASH and health interventions requires coordinated engagement from multiple sectors and stakeholders at the national level. This guideline section outlines the approach to stakeholder coordination with a focus on establishing mechanisms for collaborative planning, implementation, and monitoring of integrated WASH and health interventions. Such coordination is particularly critical during health emergencies where water-borne diseases or sanitation-related outbreaks require swift, coordinated action across sectors.

1.2.1 Stakeholder identification checklist

The eight key stakeholder categories that should be involved in the national WASH and health multi-stakeholder platform:

1. government authorities
2. humanitarian organizations
3. community representatives
4. private sector entities
5. academic institutions
6. UN agencies and donors

7. inter-cluster coordination bodies
8. professional associations and networks.

1.2.2 Strengthening meaningful participation

For effective national WASH and health coordination during emergencies, it is essential to allocate dedicated seats for community representatives, local civil society organizations, and academic institutions in coordination groups and decision-making bodies. Establishing formal partnership agreements or memoranda of understanding (MOUs) with research and training institutions will support evidence-based approaches through capacity building, data analysis, and knowledge-sharing activities. The coordination platform should employ participatory approaches that actively involve community members, including vulnerable and marginalized groups, in needs assessments, solution development, and decision-making processes. This ensures their voices are heard and their specific needs are addressed in the national response strategy. Dedicating specific seats for community representatives, women's organizations, and advocates for at-risk groups in WASH and health coordination bodies will amplify their perspectives and help address the unique challenges faced by different population segments during health emergencies, ultimately strengthening the health system's resilience.

1.2.3 Coordination mechanisms

Critical action summary

Critical action	*Timeframe*	*Lead responsibility*
Activate national WASH/health coordination platform	Within 48 hours	National government with UNICEF/WHO support
Convene initial stakeholder meeting	Within 48 hours	Platform co-chairs
Create WASH coordination task force	By day 5	Local authority and international NGO co-chairs
Complete basic 4W (who, what, where, when) mapping	First 72 hours	Information management team
Develop operational stakeholder map	By day 7	WASH coordination task force
Establish coordination function in senior ministry	By day 14	Government leadership

1.2.4 Coordination activation and structure

Action: Activate the national WASH/health coordination platform within 48 hours

Summary of key stakeholder roles

Stakeholder	*Coordination role*	*Implementation role*
Ministry of Health	Co-lead national platform; chair health sector meetings	WASH in health facility standards; staff training on WASH-IPC
WASH cluster/ lead agency	Technical coordination; information management	Emergency WASH service delivery; capacity building
WHO	Health technical guidance; disease surveillance integration	Health system strengthening; emergency health response
Local government	Subnational coordination; resource mobilization	Service delivery oversight; community engagement
NGO partners	Field-level coordination; community liaison	Direct service implementation; community mobilization

Lead: National government with WASH cluster and WHO support

Key steps:

- Establish/activate a platform co-led by the national government in collaboration with UNICEF and WHO.
- Convene an initial stakeholder meeting within 48 hours.
- Define the terms of reference based on Inter-Agency Standing Committee (IASC) reference documents and the local context (see Annex 1, section 1.2).
- Ensure the participation of key stakeholders (see Annex 1, section 1.1).

1.2.5 Establish a WASH coordination task force

Action: Create a WASH coordination task force with a clear composition and mandate

Lead: National authority and international NGO co-chairs

Task force composition:

- Relevant government ministries and agencies.
- UN agencies (UNICEF, WHO).

- International and local NGOs, including assessment specialists.
- Donor agencies.
- Private sector partners.

Core responsibilities:

- Clearly define roles for each member (see Annex 1, section 1.5).
- Ensure participatory decision-making.
- Hold regular meetings to share updates and address challenges.
- Develop information-sharing protocols between WASH and health actors.
- Ensure compliance with data protection policies.

1.2.6 Formalizing roles and responsibilities

Action: Implement a layered approach to formalizing stakeholder roles

Lead: WASH coordination task force

Rapid formalization process:

- Start with simple one-page agreements in the initial emergency phase.
- Progress to more comprehensive agreements as the situation stabilizes.
- Prioritize documenting verbal agreements through meeting minutes.

1.2.7 Institutional coordination mechanisms

Action: Establish a dedicated coordination function within senior ministry

Lead: Government leadership with support from UN agencies

Key steps:

- Place a coordination function within senior ministry (e.g. planning or finance) to:
  - facilitate inter-ministerial cooperation
  - align WASH and health coordination with national development plans
  - mobilize resources and track spending
  - ensure high-level oversight and accountability.

Coordination team composition:

- Include dedicated staff with expertise in:
  - WASH and health
  - stakeholder engagement
  - programme management
  - M&E.

1.2.8 Policy review and updates

Action: Conduct a comprehensive policy review to strengthen the coordination framework

Lead: Senior government officials with a technical support team

Key steps:

- Assess how the existing frameworks define roles, service standards, and budgeting processes for WASH and health services.
- Engage stakeholders through consultations to document gaps, overlaps, and contradictions in existing policies.
- Form a technical working group to develop actionable recommendations for policy harmonization.
- Prepare policy briefs for decision-makers and support the development of updated frameworks.

1.2.9 Monitoring, evaluation, and adaptive management

Action: Establish robust monitoring systems for integrated WASH and health outcomes

Lead: WASH and health sector monitoring specialists

Key steps:

- Track key indicators: sanitation coverage and use, WASH infrastructure functionality, fecal sludge management, household WASH expenditure, and health outcomes linked to WASH.
- Integrate all WASH health indicators with the national health management information system (HMIS) from day 1,

ensuring compatibility with disease surveillance and health facility reporting systems.

- Establish data sharing protocols with Ministry of Health information managers using national health data standards.

1.2.10 Cross-sectoral coordination

Action: Implement strategies for effective cross-sectoral coordination

Lead: WASH and health sector leads with support from coordination specialists

Key steps:

- Coordinate hygiene promotion with community mobilization strategies across sectors.
- Ensure at-risk groups are represented in coordination mechanisms.
- Establish referral pathways between WASH actors, healthcare facilities, and other sectors (nutrition, shelter, protection).
- Develop joint technical working groups with shared standards and cross-training.
- Create integrated work plans with joint monitoring for cross-cutting activities.

1.2.11 Community engagement and participation

Action: Establish mechanisms for meaningful community engagement in coordination

Lead: WASH and health sector leads with community engagement specialists

Key steps:

- Map existing community structures and actively engage local leaders and community-based organizations.
- Reserve seats for community representatives in coordination bodies.
- Create accessible communication channels for diverse groups, including regular consultation sessions.

- Establish transparent feedback mechanisms and track responses to community input.
- Build the capacity of local organizations for effective advocacy.

1.3 Emergency WASH actions

The emergency WASH actions outlined in this section provide a framework for rapid response in the acute phase of a crisis, focusing on the first 90 days. The emergency actions (days 0–14) prioritize life-saving interventions, while the resilience actions (days 14–90) emphasize sustainability and resilience. Key actions include rapid assessments, ensuring access to safe water and sanitation, promoting hygiene, controlling disease vectors, and coordinating with the health sector. The section also guides the review and strengthening of public health policies and the transition to community-managed WASH services.

1.3.1 Emergency actions (days 0–14)

The emergency actions phase (days 0–14) is crucial for mitigating public health risks and preventing disease outbreaks during a humanitarian crisis. Rapid assessments are conducted to identify areas with the greatest health and sanitation strengths and needs, focusing on the status of healthcare facilities, water and sanitation infrastructure, and hygiene practices. Key activities include ensuring access to safe water and sanitation in healthcare settings, distributing essential hygiene and cleaning supplies, and promoting infection prevention and control measures. Coordination with health actors is prioritized to align WASH interventions with disease surveillance data, treatment protocols, and community health promotion efforts. The emergency actions set the stage for more comprehensive, health-focused WASH interventions in the subsequent phases of the emergency, aiming to protect and improve public health outcomes.

1.3.1.1 Rapidly assess WASH strengths and needs

Timing: Begin the assessment within the first 72 hours of the emergency and complete the initial rapid assessment within 14 days.

Key steps:

1. Use existing standardized tools to identify areas and populations with the greatest health and sanitation needs and risks.
2. Conduct a multisectoral assessment, engaging experts from relevant fields and backgrounds, drawing on infection prevention and control frameworks and best practices.
3. Gather qualitative data on cultural practices, social norms, and power dynamics influencing WASH access and outcomes by engaging community representatives and local organizations.
4. Rapidly analyse and disseminate assessment findings to inform community-level response planning and resource allocation.
5. Use harmonized questions and indicators from the WHO/UNICEF JMP to ensure comparability and alignment with global standards.

1.3.1.2 Ensure access to safe and sufficient water

Timing: Provide minimum safe water quantities within the first 72 hours and progressively increase access and quality throughout the first 14 days of the response.

Key steps:

1. Mobilize and deploy water trucking, treatment kits, storage receptacles, and purification supplies to affected areas, prioritizing the most vulnerable groups.
2. Set up and manage water trucking services in coordination with community members, ensuring equitable distribution and accessibility for all.
3. Test water quality at both the source and point of use, and treat and protect water sources to maintain safety standards.
4. Ensure minimum water quantities are met, providing at least:
   - 5 litres per person per day for outpatients
   - 40–60 litres per person per day for inpatients in health facilities
   - 15 litres per person per day at the household level.
5. Monitor and maintain water quality, with free residual chlorine levels of 0.2–0.5 mg/litre at the point of delivery.

1.3.1.3 Ensure safe and acceptable sanitation facilities

Timing: Provide basic, shared sanitation facilities within the first 72 hours and progressively increase access to safe, acceptable, and sustainable facilities throughout the first 14 days and beyond.

Key steps:

1. Coordinate with gender-based violence counterparts to install gender-segregated emergency latrines in public places, such as camps, schools, markets, and health facilities, aiming for a maximum of 50 people per latrine.
2. Construct temporary household latrines and support the rapid repair of existing toilets using locally available materials and designs.
3. Distribute culturally appropriate, gender-sensitive hygiene and menstrual health management kits to support the use and maintenance of sanitation facilities.
4. Promote community engagement in selecting sanitation technologies, siting facilities, and establishing operations and maintenance systems to ensure acceptability and sustainability.
5. Ensure the accessibility and safety of sanitation facilities for women, girls, people with disabilities, and other vulnerable groups through inclusive design and siting.

1.3.1.4 Promote key hygiene practices

Timing: Begin hygiene promotion activities within the first 72 hours of the response and sustain them throughout the emergency and recovery phases.

Key steps:

1. Distribute context-appropriate and gender-sensitive hygiene kits, including soap, water containers, and menstrual hygiene and incontinence materials, to affected households.
2. Focus hygiene promotion on key behaviours that prevent disease transmission, such as handwashing at critical times, safe water handling, and food hygiene.
3. Launch community-level hygiene promotion campaigns using multiple channels, such as radio, posters, and interpersonal communication, to maximize reach and reinforce messages.

4. Target hygiene promotion to high-risk groups, such as caregivers of young children, elderly people, and people with disabilities, using tailored behaviour change approaches and communication methods.
5. Train community health workers, volunteers, and hygiene promoters on effective behaviour change techniques, including demonstrations, storytelling, and problem solving.

1.3.1.5 Control vector breeding and transmission

Timing: Assess vector risks and implement control measures within the first 14 days of the response, and sustain efforts throughout the emergency and recovery phases.

Key steps:

1. Mobilize community members to identify and eliminate mosquito breeding sites by removing standing water and safely disposing of solid waste.
2. In coordination with health actors, distribute long-lasting insecticide-treated nets to affected households and promote their correct and consistent use.
3. Implement safe and effective chemical and biological vector control measures, such as indoor residual spraying and larviciding, in consultation with the community and relevant experts.
4. Establish community-based vector surveillance systems to monitor the presence and density of mosquitoes and other disease vectors, and to guide the targeting and adaptation of control interventions.
5. Promote the safe storage and handling of drinking water and food to prevent contamination by vectors and pests using locally appropriate and affordable container covers and storage methods.

1.3.1.6 Establish health sector coordination mechanisms

Timing: Establish coordination mechanisms with health actors within the first 72 hours of the response, and maintain regular communication and collaboration throughout the emergency and recovery phases.

Key steps:

1. Assess WASH-related disease risks and identify high-vulnerability groups, such as children under five, pregnant women, people with disabilities, older persons, and people with compromised immune systems, in coordination with health experts.
2. Establish community-level joint surveillance and referral systems to enable the early detection, reporting, and control of WASH-related disease outbreaks, in collaboration with community health workers and volunteers.
3. Provide essential WASH facilities, supplies, and services at community health centres, oral rehydration points, and other frontline care delivery sites, in accordance with healthcare protocols and standards.
4. Map and strengthen the capacity of community-based health workforces to promote hygiene, deliver WASH-related health messages, and facilitate community engagement and participation in WASH interventions.
5. Establish and maintain clear referral pathways and communication channels between community health facilities and WASH service providers to ensure a timely and coordinated response to WASH-related health issues.

1.3.1.7 Review and strengthen public health sanitation policies

Timing: Conduct a rapid review of the existing sanitation policies within the first 14 days of the response, and support policy-strengthening efforts throughout the emergency and recovery phases.

Key steps:

1. Assess the comprehensiveness, clarity, and coherence of local sanitation legislation and standards along the entire sanitation service chain, from containment to treatment and safe disposal or reuse.
2. Identify policy gaps, inconsistencies, and implementation challenges that may hinder the effectiveness, equity, and sustainability of emergency sanitation interventions.
3. Ensure that sanitation policy frameworks are evidence based, assign clear institutional roles and responsibilities, and include provisions for community participation and accountability.

4. Support the development or revision of emergency-specific sanitation policies and protocols to enable the rapid deployment of context-appropriate interventions in future crises.
5. Use policy review findings to inform the design and adaptation of emergency sanitation strategies and to advocate for longer-term policy reforms and investments in resilient sanitation systems.

1.3.1.8 Establish realistic and incremental sanitation standards

Timing: Establish initial minimum sanitation standards within the first 14 days of the response, and progressively raise standards throughout the emergency and recovery phases as conditions allow.

Key steps:

1. Base initial sanitation standards on a rapid assessment of public health risks, existing sanitation access and practices, and available resources and capacities on the ground.
2. Ensure that sanitation standards are aligned with global humanitarian guidelines, such as the Sphere standards, while being adapted to the local context and emergency phase.
3. Engage affected communities in setting and monitoring sanitation standards, ensuring that their needs, preferences, and constraints are reflected in the design and management of facilities and services.
4. Encourage the use of locally appropriate, affordable, and sustainable sanitation technologies and approaches that can be easily operated and maintained by communities.
5. Establish mechanisms for the regular review and adjustment of sanitation standards based on evolving needs, capacities, and lessons learned throughout the emergency and recovery phases.

1.3.2 Resilience actions (days 14–90)

The resilience actions phase (days 14–90) focuses on strengthening the resilience and sustainability of emergency WASH interventions by engaging and empowering local actors, systems, and resources. This phase prioritizes capacity building, community-led management, and alignment with long-term development goals. Case Study 2.2 in the full text (Yemen: Evidence-based water management in conflict zones) showcases how the International Organization for Migration partnered with local authorities and technical experts to conduct groundwater assessments and develop sustainable water management strategies, demonstrating the importance of integrating local knowledge and capacity into emergency response efforts.

1.3.2.1 Strengthen local WASH capacity and resources

Timing: Begin capacity and resource assessments within the first 14 days of the response, and continue strengthening efforts throughout the emergency, recovery, and development phases.

Key steps:

1. Pre-position essential WASH and health supplies in strategic locations, in collaboration with local authorities and partners, to enable rapid deployment and distribution in case of an emergency.
2. Work with local partners to map, mobilize, and strengthen community-based WASH infrastructure, supply chains, and market systems, leveraging existing resources and capacities.
3. Engage community leaders and representatives in all aspects of the emergency WASH response, from planning and implementation to monitoring and evaluation, to ensure local ownership and sustainability.
4. Identify opportunities to support the development and expansion of local WASH market systems, including through capacity building, financial assistance, and public–private partnerships.

1.3.2.2 Initiate community-based WASH training and capacity building

Timing: Initiate community-based training and capacity building within the first 30 days of the response, and continue to provide ongoing learning and support throughout the emergency, recovery, and development phases.

Key steps:

1. Train local authorities, WASH service providers, and community-based health, education, and nutrition workers on key WASH topics, such as water safety, sanitation management, and hygiene promotion.
2. Strengthen the governance and coordination capacities of local WASH institutions and platforms, such as water user associations, sanitation committees, and multi-stakeholder forums.
3. Promote household water treatment and safe storage practices, using locally available materials and technologies, and building on existing community knowledge and preferences.
4. Shift from one-off, classroom-based training sessions to ongoing, on-the-job mentoring, peer learning, and experiential capacity-building approaches that are tailored to local needs and contexts.

1.3.2.3 Transition to community-managed, climate-resilient WASH services

Timing: Initiate the transition to community-managed, climate-resilient WASH services within the first 90 days of the response, and continue to support and monitor the process throughout the recovery and development phases.

Key steps:

1. Support the participatory development and implementation of community-level water and sanitation safety plans that identify and mitigate key risks and vulnerabilities, including those related to climate change.
2. Facilitate inclusive, community-led planning processes for the design, construction, and management of sustainable, climate-resilient WASH infrastructure and services.
3. Establish community-based monitoring, feedback, and accountability mechanisms to ensure that WASH services are responsive to local needs, preferences, and grievances, and are adapted to evolving climatic conditions.
4. Provide ongoing technical, financial, and institutional support to community-based WASH service providers and management structures to ensure the long-term functionality, quality, and equity of services.

1.3.2.4 Initiate emergency WASH and long-term development alignment

Timing: Initiate the alignment of emergency WASH interventions with long-term development within the first 30 days of the response, and continue to update and adapt alignment strategies throughout the recovery and development phases.

Key steps:

1. Review existing local and national WASH policies, budgets, and strategies to identify opportunities for alignment with emergency WASH priorities, approaches, and standards.
2. Advocate for the integration of climate-resilient, risk-informed, and inclusive WASH approaches and technologies into long-term development plans and investments.
3. Promote participatory, accountable, and transparent WASH governance mechanisms that engage affected communities, particularly marginalized and vulnerable groups, in decision-making and oversight.
4. Establish and strengthen strategic partnerships between humanitarian and development actors, including the government, civil society, and the private sector, to leverage comparative advantages and ensure a coordinated, sustainable WASH response.

1.3.2.5 Establish WASH outcomes monitoring and evaluation

Timing: Establish WASH monitoring and evaluation systems within the first 30 days of the response, and continue to collect, analyse, and use data throughout the emergency, recovery, and development phases.

Key steps:

1. Develop and implement a comprehensive monitoring and evaluation framework that tracks the coverage, quality, and use of WASH services, using both quantitative and qualitative indicators and methods.
2. Assess the short-term and long-term impacts of WASH interventions on key outcomes, such as hygiene behaviour change,

disease reduction, and community resilience, using rigorous research and evaluation designs.
3. Strengthen the capacity of local WASH institutions and service providers to collect, analyse, and use monitoring and evaluation data for planning, management, and accountability purposes.
4. Use participatory monitoring and evaluation tools and approaches to gather real-time feedback from affected communities and ensure that WASH interventions are responsive to their needs, preferences, and concerns.
5. Establish clear benchmarks and targets for progressive improvements in WASH outcomes, and use monitoring and evaluation data to identify and prioritize corrective actions and adaptations.

1.3.2.6 Initiate lessons learned documentation and sharing

Timing: Initiate the documentation and sharing of lessons learned within the first 90 days of the response, and continue to update and disseminate learning throughout the emergency, recovery, and development phases.

Key steps:

1. Capture and synthesize the perspectives and experiences of affected communities on the effectiveness, relevance, and sustainability of WASH interventions, using participatory assessment and feedback tools.
2. Facilitate cross-learning and knowledge exchange between communities, agencies, and sectors through peer-to-peer learning events, workshops, and online platforms.
3. Document and disseminate best practices, innovations, and lessons learned from emergency WASH interventions through case studies, guidance notes, and other knowledge products.
4. Advocate for the integration of community-based, locally led WASH approaches and learning into national and global policies, strategies, and programmes.
5. Establish and maintain repositories, networks, and communities of practice to enable the long-term access, use, and updating of WASH lessons learned and best practices.

1.4 Monitoring

1.4.1 Key monitoring activities

1.4.1.1 Engaging communities

Community participation is vital for relevant, context-specific monitoring. Affected people should be actively involved in designing indicators, collecting data, analysing results, and planning improvements.

- Consult diverse community members to identify locally appropriate indicators and involve them in participatory data collection and analysis.
- Establish community feedback mechanisms and dashboards to support local decision-making and accountability.
- Ensure data are disaggregated by sex, age, disability, and other vulnerability characteristics.
- Triangulate findings using household surveys, facility assessments, and community scorecards.

1.4.1.2 Harmonizing indicators and systems

Standardized frameworks enable coherent data collection and use across WASH and health actors, aligned with national systems and global standards.

- Develop a core set of WASH-health indicators for emergencies aligned with national frameworks and Sustainable Development Goal (SDG)/WHO/UNICEF JMP standards.
- Integrate key indicators into WASH and health information management systems at all levels.
- Establish data sharing and protection protocols to enable joint analysis.

1.4.1.3 Strengthening community capacities

Building local monitoring skills is key for ownership, sustainability, and resilience.

- Train community teams on WASH and health monitoring using simple, practical methods.
- Mentor health facility staff to routinely monitor WASH services and practices.

- Establish community-managed monitoring systems for WASH facilities and behaviours.
- Strengthen local government capacities for WASH-health data management and use.

1.4.1.4 Utilizing monitoring data

Regular review and use of monitoring data drives evidence-based action to improve quality, coverage, and equity of WASH-health interventions.

- Analyse monitoring data to assess WASH-health service functionality, quality, and utilization.
- Produce user-friendly dashboards and reports to inform decision-making and advocacy.
- Convene joint data review meetings with communities, health actors, and local authorities.
- Use community WASH monitoring data in local health and development planning and budgeting processes.

1.4.2 Key monitoring indicators

WASH and health monitoring indicators track the inputs, outputs, and outcomes of integrated programming.

Domain	*Key indicators*
WASH in health facilities	Proportion of health facilities with functional WASH services meeting national standards; proportion of staff trained on WASH-IPC protocols.
Outbreak detection and response	Number and timeliness of suspected outbreak alerts investigated; proportion of outbreak response plans with integrated WASH-health interventions.
Hygiene and health behaviours	Proportion of households with handwashing facilities with soap and water; proportion practising safe drinking water and food hygiene behaviours.
WASH-related disease burden	Incidence rates of priority WASH-related diseases (e.g. cholera, hepatitis E); morbidity and mortality rates disaggregated by age and sex.
Community access and functionality	Percentage of households with access to safely managed drinking water and sanitation; number of days water points and sanitation facilities are non-functional.

1.4.3 Monitoring methods and tools

- Health facility assessments (e.g. WASH FIT, IPC scorecards) and service quality spot checks.
- Community-based disease surveillance and outbreak investigation reports.
- Household surveys on WASH access, quality, use, and health behaviours.
- HMIS data on WASH-related disease trends.
- Standardized tools and templates adapted to local context from global quality assurance frameworks.

1.4.4 Monitoring roles and responsibilities

Actor	*Key responsibilities*
Community actors	Participate in defining local monitoring priorities; collect and report data on community WASH-health behaviours and outcomes; co-lead monitoring efforts through community-based working groups.
Implementing agencies	Coordinate harmonized monitoring systems; train staff and partners on data collection and analysis; compile and disseminate data for decision-making and advocacy.
Government counterparts	Oversee WASH-health monitoring at national and subnational levels; integrate indicators into epidemiological and early warning systems; use monitoring data to inform preparedness, response planning, and resourcing.

1.4.5 Monitoring timeline and deliverables

Frequency	*Activity*
Acute phase + periodic	Rapid WASH-health assessments.
Monthly	Reporting of WASH and health data from facilities and communities.
Quarterly	Analysis and dissemination of monitoring trends and performance.
Annually	Joint review meetings and learning workshops on WASH-health coordination.

Key deliverables:

- WASH-health assessment and surveillance database, dashboards, and reports.
- Monitoring framework, methods, and tools for emergencies.
- Outbreak investigation and after-action review reports.
- Community-specific bulletins distilling key data and trends.

CHAPTER 2

Brief 2. Integration in emergencies

Guideline for coordinating WASH with nutrition at the national level

Source document: Chapter 3 in Sorensen, Nikolas, Mariëlle Snel, James Ray III, and Syed Yasir Ahmad Khan. 2026. *Building Resilience: Coordination Guidelines for Integrated WASH, Health, and Nutrition Programming in Crisis Settings*. Practical Action Publishing. http://doi.org/10.3362/9781788534710

2.1 Executive summary

This guideline provides essential guidance on coordination for national officials overseeing WASH and nutrition initiatives during emergencies. It supports rapid response while emphasizing long-term resilience, serving as one of four complementary guidelines designed as an integrated framework for WASH coordination with health and nutrition at both national and community levels. This guideline was developed by the WASH Road Map in consultation with numerous other professionals.

2.1.1 Purpose

This guideline helps national-level officials and humanitarian coordinators integrate WASH and nutrition interventions during emergencies through structured, time-bound actions. It operationalizes a multisectoral approach to addressing the underlying causes of undernutrition, particularly during the critical first 1,000 days from conception to a child's second birthday. It upholds the rights outlined in the Humanitarian Charter and aligns with global commitments to advance universal health coverage and primary healthcare.

2.1.2 Key actions

Actions	*WASH*	*Nutrition*	*Timeframe*	*Guideline sections*	*Practitioners' Toolkit sections*
Establish community WASH and nutrition committee	Identify WASH representatives and define roles	Identify nutrition representatives and define roles	Within 48 hours	2.2.4, 2.2.5	1.1, 1.2
Conduct participatory community mapping and assessment	Assess WASH conditions, practices, and map community structures	Assess nutrition status, conduct rapid nutrition assessment practices, and map existing nutrition services	Days 1–5	2.2.5, 2.2.7, 2.3.1.1	1.3, 1.4, 2.1, 2.2, 2.3
Provide emergency WASH interventions integrated with nutrition	Ensure access to safe WASH; integrate WASH into nutrition service delivery points	Support nutrition-sensitive WASH interventions; integrate WASH messages into nutrition programming	Days 1–14	2.3.1.2, 2.3.1.3	2.1, 2.2, 2.3, 4.1, 4.4, 4.6, 4.10
Develop joint strategies and communication systems	Contribute to integrated strategy development; set up WASH feedback systems	Contribute to integrated strategy development; set up nutrition feedback systems	Days 5–14	2.2.8, 2.2.9, 2.3.1.4	3.1, 3.2, 5.3

(*Continues*)

(Continued)

Actions	*WASH*	*Nutrition*	*Timeframe*	*Guideline sections*	*Practitioners' Toolkit sections*
Establish integrated monitoring and community coordination	Develop WASH indicators aligned with nutrition outcomes; support community coordination functions	Adapt nutrition indicators that capture WASH-sensitive measures; support community monitoring	Days 14–30	2.2.9, 2.3.1.4, 2.4	1.2, 3.3, 4.8, 4.9, 5.1, 5.3, 5.5
Mobilize community champions and expand to schools	Engage WASH champions and promote WASH in schools integrated with nutrition education	Engage nutrition champions and promote nutrition education in schools integrated with WASH	Days 14–60	2.2.9, 2.3.2.2	3.3, 4.2, 4.3, 4.4, 4.7
Strengthen local capacity and build sustainable partnerships	Build sustainable WASH capacity, forge partnerships, and plan transition strategies	Build sustainable nutrition capacity, develop partnerships, and plan for sustainability	Days 30–90	2.2.10, 2.3.2.1, 2.3.2.3	1.3, 1.4, 3.4, 3.6

2.1.3 Framework pillars

These five pillars structure the detailed guidance found throughout this guideline:

1. *National coordination*: Establish inclusive mechanisms across ministries, nutrition/WASH actors, and development partners.
2. *Strategic assessment*: Identify critical WASH–nutrition links, vulnerability patterns, and existing national capacities.
3. *Integrated service delivery*: Address immediate WASH and nutrition needs while strengthening national food and water systems.
4. *National capacity building*: Develop sustainable government and partner capacity for nutrition-sensitive WASH programming.
5. *National monitoring*: Track integrated WASH-nutrition outcomes to ensure accountability, facilitate learning, and inform future strategies.

This guideline integrates climate resilience, protection, gender equity, and social inclusion while clarifying roles across government, humanitarian, and community actors. It bridges emergency response and long-term development at the national level.

2.2 Stakeholder coordination

Effective stakeholder coordination is essential for the successful integration of WASH and nutrition interventions at the national level. This guideline establishes a framework for engaging all relevant actors in planning, implementation, and monitoring activities across eight critical stakeholder categories: government authorities, humanitarian and development organizations, community and civil society representatives, private sector entities, academic and research institutions, UN agencies and donors, inter-cluster coordination mechanisms and professional associations and networks. While numerous stakeholders contribute to this coordination platform, particular attention should be given to securing participation from both nutrition-focused and WASH-oriented entities to create an integrated approach, addressing the complex relationship between WASH practices and nutritional outcomes.

2.2.1 Stakeholder identification checklist

There are eight key stakeholder categories that should be involved in the WASH and nutrition multi-stakeholder platform at the national level. Each category of stakeholders is essential for comprehensive emergency response.

1. government authorities
2. humanitarian organizations
3. community representatives
4. private sector entities
5. academic institutions
6. UN agencies and donors
7. inter-cluster coordination bodies
8. professional associations and networks

2.2.2 Strengthening meaningful participation

To enhance the effectiveness of the national WASH and nutrition coordination platform, priority should be given to allocating dedicated seats for community representatives, local civil society organizations, and local academic institutions in coordination groups and decision-making bodies. Formal partnership agreements or MOUs with research and training institutions are recommended to support capacity building, data analysis, and knowledge-sharing activities. The coordination mechanism should implement participatory approaches that actively involve community members – including vulnerable and marginalized groups such as women's organizations and disability advocates – in needs assessments, solution development, and decision-making processes. Engaging this diverse range of stakeholders, especially those most affected by the crisis, is essential to ensuring an inclusive, effective, and locally relevant humanitarian response that addresses the complex interrelationship between WASH factors and nutritional outcomes at the national level.

2.2.3 Coordination mechanisms

Critical action summary

Critical action	*Timeframe*	*Lead responsibility*
Activate national coordination platform	Within 48 hours	Government ministries with UNICEF/cluster support

(Continues)

(Continued)

Critical action	*Timeframe*	*Lead responsibility*
Convene initial multi-stakeholder meeting	Within 48 hours	Platform co-chairs
Establish WASH-nutrition task force	By day 5	Platform co-chairs
Complete rapid stakeholder assessment	Days 1–3	Information management officer
Develop a comprehensive stakeholder matrix	By day 14	Information management team
Develop joint, multi-year response plan	By day 30	WASH-nutrition task force

2.2.4 Coordination activation and structure

Action: Establish a national WASH and nutrition coordination platform within 48 hours

Summary of key stakeholder roles

Stakeholder	*Coordination role*	*Implementation role*
Ministry of Health/Nutrition	Co-lead national platform; chair nutrition sector meetings	Nutrition service standards; integration of WASH in nutrition protocols
WASH cluster/lead agency	Technical coordination; information management	Emergency WASH service delivery; water quality and hygiene promotion
UNICEF	Nutrition technical leadership; inter-agency coordination	Nutrition programming; WASH-nutrition integration support
World Food Programme	Food assistance coordination; supply chain management	Food distribution; nutrition programme implementation
Local government	Subnational coordination; resource mobilization	Service delivery oversight; community nutrition programmes
NGO partners	Field-level coordination; community liaison	Direct service implementation; community-based nutrition programmes
Community health workers	Local coordination; outreach coordination	Integrated nutrition and hygiene counselling; community screening

Lead: Government ministries (WASH, health, nutrition) with WASH/nutrition cluster/sector support

Key steps:

- Determine the appropriate coordination mechanism (standalone or integrated into existing structures).
- Establish co-leadership between government ministries and UNICEF/cluster or sector lead agencies.
- Ensure reporting lines to the WASH cluster or sector coordinator and the UN Office for the Coordination of Humanitarian Affairs (OCHA) inter-cluster coordinator, who relay information to the humanitarian coordinator/humanitarian country team.
- Formalize the reporting lines through inclusive terms of reference that align with IASC cluster coordination guidelines while adapting to the local context.

2.2.5 Stakeholder engagement and meeting management

Action: Convene a multi-stakeholder coordination meeting within 48 hours

Lead: Platform co-chairs

Key steps:

- Establish a shared understanding of the situation, WASH/nutrition linkages, needs, and capacities.
- Agree on joint priorities, objectives, and response strategies.
- Define inclusive decision-making processes and working methods.
- Ensure balanced representation across all stakeholder groups.

2.2.6 Technical coordination structures

Action: Establish technical and operational coordination mechanisms

Lead: Platform co-chairs

Key components and responsibilities

Structure	*Role*
WASH-nutrition task force	Joint assessments, integrated response plans, technical guidance (government, UN, NGOs, research)

(*Continues*)

(Continued)

Structure	*Role*
Strategic advisory group	Strategic decision-making, response planning, implementation oversight
Technical working groups	Address specific technical challenges, develop standards (time bound)
Subnational platforms	Localized implementation aligned with national strategy, clear reporting lines
Information management team	Data collection, analysis, and visualization

2.2.7 Stakeholder mapping and management

Action: Develop and maintain a comprehensive stakeholder mapping system

Lead: Information management officer

Timeline:

- Days 1–3: rapid 4W mapping → day 14: comprehensive matrix → ongoing: regular updates.

Stakeholders: Government ministries, UN agencies/clusters, NGOs, civil society, community organizations, donors, private sector, and academic institutions

Responsibilities:

- Information management officer: maintain database and visualizations.
- Coordination team: lead joint crisis planning discussions.
- Sector leads: analyse data to identify gaps and opportunities.
- All partners: provide regular activity and capacity updates.

2.2.8 Policy alignment and joint planning

Action: Conduct a policy review and develop a joint response plan

Lead: WASH and nutrition task force

Policy review: Review existing sectoral policies to identify gaps and integration opportunities; ensure WASH is prioritized as a determinant of nutrition outcomes; clarify institutional roles and accountability mechanisms.

Joint response plan requirements:

- Time-bound, measurable objectives with clear roles and responsibilities.
- Sequenced, adaptable interventions aligned with national policies and emergency frameworks.

Planning process: Base the plan on the policy review, stakeholder mapping, and needs assessment. Ensure there is an inclusive consultation with affected communities, develop multi-year timeframes with short/long-term objectives, and include resource mobilization and sustainability considerations.

2.2.9 Monitoring, evaluation, and accountability

Action: Establish a unified information management and accountability system

Lead: Information management team with WASH and nutrition sector leads

Information management system:

- Standardized Monitoring and Assessment of Relief and Transitions (SMART) indicators for integrated WASH-nutrition outputs and outcomes.
- Alignment with ministry/UNICEF/OCHA reporting and national HMIS.
- Sex-, age-, and disability-disaggregated data.
- Regular joint analysis and information products.

Accountability mechanisms:

- Joint supervision of adherence to WASH-nutrition standards.
- Transparent tracking of funding, expenditures, and results.
- Accessible complaint and feedback mechanisms.
- Regular joint reviews and quality assurance checks.

2.2.10 Transition and sustainability

Action: Plan for a transition to sustainable coordination from the outset

Lead: Platform co-chairs with government counterparts

Key steps:

- Progressively transfer leadership to national and subnational authorities.
- Strengthen the government's capacity for multisectoral coordination.
- Empower local organizations for service delivery and monitoring.
- Provide sustainable institutional support for building local capacities.

2.3 Emergency WASH actions

The emergency WASH actions outlined in this section provide a roadmap for swift, coordinated, and context-specific interventions to address the critical WASH needs of nutritionally vulnerable populations during humanitarian crises. The framework prioritizes life-saving measures in the emergency actions phase (days 0–14), followed by a concerted effort to integrate WASH interventions with local capacity, ensuring sustainable and resilient solutions in the days 14–90 timeframe. Key actions encompass rapid joint assessments, ensuring access to sufficient quantities of safe water, providing dignified sanitation facilities, promoting critical hygiene practices, and enhancing community-driven coordination. The section also emphasizes the importance of aligning WASH strategies with nutrition sector priorities and strengthening local systems for long-term impact.

2.3.1 Emergency actions (days 0–14)

The emergency actions phase (days 0–14) is critical for addressing the most pressing WASH needs of nutritionally vulnerable populations during a humanitarian crisis. Rapid joint assessments are conducted in collaboration with nutrition actors to identify areas and groups with the highest risk of malnutrition, focusing on the availability and accessibility of safe WASH services. Key activities include ensuring access to sufficient quantities of safe water for drinking and cooking, providing gender-sensitive sanitation facilities, distributing hygiene kits tailored to the needs of families with young children, and promoting key hygiene practices that prevent the spread of diarrheal diseases. Coordination with nutrition actors is prioritized to align WASH interventions with programmes that manage acute malnutrition, support infant and young child feeding, and other nutrition-specific interventions. The emergency actions lay the foundation for more targeted, nutrition-sensitive WASH interventions in the subsequent phases of the emergency, aiming to protect and improve the nutritional status of vulnerable populations.

2.3.1.1 Conduct rapid joint WASH and nutrition assessment

Timing: Within the first 14 days of the emergency response.

Key steps:

1. Identify high-risk populations, existing community structures, and resources (coordinate with the nutrition cluster, community representatives, and local sectors).
2. Review primary and secondary data on local capabilities, crisis impact, WASH/health/nutrition outcomes, and cultural beliefs/practices.
3. Conduct joint, multisector rapid assessments at the community level with diverse participation to understand local strengths and needs.
4. Engage the community as active participants throughout the assessment process.
5. Share findings with community members and local partners to inform locally acceptable, sustainable interventions.

2.3.1.2 Conduct life-saving, community-based WASH interventions

Timing: Within the first 14 days of the emergency response.

Key steps:

1. *Water supply*: support a community-led rehabilitation of water sources, provide household treatment/storage options, promote

water safety planning, and implement temporary solutions (kiosks, water trucking) based on community preferences.

2. *Sanitation*: construct communal latrines using local designs/labour, install gender-segregated and secure toilets, adapt facilities for vulnerable users, and establish community-led maintenance systems.
3. *Hygiene promotion*: engage community actors for behaviour change, co-design and distribute handwashing stations/hygiene kits, conduct promotion at key sites, and integrate hygiene messages into existing health/nutrition programming.
4. *Safe food handling*: promote hygienic food preparation and storage, distribute cooking/storage supplies, and train food handlers with community authority oversight.
5. *Prioritize vulnerable groups*: target pregnant and lactating women, children under five, malnourished families, marginalized households, and individuals with health conditions affecting WASH and nutrition.
6. *Community action plan*: jointly develop a plan with community-defined targets, leverage local resources, outline implementation/monitoring roles, and establish shared progress indicators.

2.3.1.3 Integrate WASH into community-based nutrition programmes

Timing: Start integrating WASH within the first 14 days of the emergency response and continue throughout the programme cycle.

Key steps:

1. *Integrated community activities*: engage health workers, volunteers, and peer educators in joint household visits, cooking/hygiene sessions, dialogues, and malnutrition screening/referral.
2. *Community-led infrastructure*: build WASH facilities at nutrition sites using local labour; establish community committees and cost sharing for ownership and maintenance.
3. *Behaviour change communication*: partner with local leaders and influencers to develop culturally adapted materials and messaging in local languages.

2.3.1.4 Strengthen community-driven coordination

Timing: Establish within 14 days; strengthen through response and recovery.

Key steps:

1. *Coordination*: regular multisector community meetings to set goals, target marginalized groups, and solve problems collectively.
2. *Feedback*: accessible accountability mechanisms (hotlines, scorecards, participatory reviews) informed by community input.
3. *Monitoring*: joint indicators and participatory tools; regular reviews to track progress and plan corrective actions.

2.3.2 Resilience actions (days 14–90)

Integrating emergency WASH interventions with local capacity is crucial for building resilience and ensuring the sustainability of nutrition-sensitive WASH services beyond the acute crisis phase. This section focuses on the days 14–90 timeframe, wherein concerted efforts are made to engage, strengthen, and empower local actors, systems, and resources. Key strategies include assessing and building the capacity of local WASH and nutrition stakeholders, mobilizing community structures and champions, forging partnerships for resilience, and facilitating a smooth transition to community-managed, climate-resilient WASH services.

2.3.2.1 Strengthen local government and community capacity

Timing: Begin within 14 days; focus on days 14–90 through recovery.

Key steps:

1. *Policy adaptation*: work with local authorities to review and adapt policies through participatory analysis, embed community priorities into official guidance, and advocate for increased funding and decentralized support for community-led WASH-nutrition programming.

2. *Workforce capacity*: train government staff as master trainers, create peer-learning and mentorship networks, and develop simple tools and job aids for frontline workers to promote integrated behaviours.
3. *Multi-year planning*: support communities to develop costed WASH-nutrition action plans through inclusive planning, local capacity/resource mapping, and technical support in budgeting, resource mobilization, and implementation.
4. *Participatory monitoring integration*: co-develop community-defined indicators and monitoring tools, build local authority capacity to manage participatory data, and advocate for inclusion in subnational and national information systems.

2.3.2.2 Mobilize community structures and champions

Timing: Identify and engage within the first 14 days; support and strengthen throughout days 14–90 and beyond.

Key steps:

1. *Engage leaders*: map and sensitize traditional, religious, and civic leaders on key WASH-nutrition issues; train them as behaviour change champions and community mobilizers.
2. *Strengthen community structures*: form or reinforce inclusive structures (WASH-nutrition committees, mother-to-mother support groups, father support groups, youth-led clubs) to lead local planning, peer education, and intergenerational behaviour change.
3. *Support champions*: use community feedback to identify role models and early adopters; provide training and incentives to engage them as peer educators and advocates within their social networks.
4. *Community-led WASH facilities*: facilitate participatory design, train local artisans in construction and maintenance, and establish systems (e.g. water user committees) to sustain services.

2.3.2.3 Forge community partnerships for resilience

Timing: Identify and engage partners within the first 30 days; strengthen throughout days 14–90 and beyond.

Key steps:

1. *Risk and preparedness planning*: train community members in participatory hazard mapping and risk assessment; facilitate analysis of WASH-nutrition vulnerabilities; develop preparedness plans with clear roles and resources for mitigating shocks.
2. *Contingency funds and stockpiles*: conduct feasibility/market assessments, train community structures in transparent fund and supply management, and provide seed funding with linkages to financial institutions for sustainability.
3. *Multi-stakeholder partnerships*: support community-led WASH-nutrition initiatives by engaging local entrepreneurs, linking savings groups to credit/livelihoods, collaborating with schools and local media, and scaling successful models through local organizations.
4. *Cross-sector coordination*: develop integrated referral protocols across health, nutrition, and WASH systems; promote cross-training among community workers; establish community-managed posts with basic WASH services; create local platforms for joint planning and accountability.

2.4 Monitoring

2.4.1 Key monitoring activities

2.4.1.1 Engaging communities

Ensure there is meaningful participation of diverse community members – including women, children, and marginalized groups – throughout monitoring.

- Train community members in context-specific WASH-nutrition assessments.
- Collaborate with representatives to select locally appropriate indicators and conduct joint analysis with accessible feedback sessions.
- Use participatory methods (household interviews, focus groups, direct observation).
- Disaggregate data by sex, age, and disability to track disparities and equitable access.

- Establish accessible feedback/complaint mechanisms (suggestions boxes, help desks, community meetings) with timely responses.

2.4.1.2 Harmonizing indicators and systems

Align monitoring with national/global frameworks while allowing context-specific flexibility.

- Develop core WASH-nutrition indicators aligned with national systems and SDGs.
- Integrate indicators into national/subnational information systems.
- Harmonize tools, methodologies, and reporting timeframes across partners.
- Establish clear roles, accountability, and data sharing protocols.
- Develop joint M&E plans with nutrition actors, defining shared indicators and follow-up mechanisms.

2.4.1.3 Strengthening community capacities

Build local capacity for sustained participatory monitoring.

- Train community-monitoring teams using simple, locally adapted tools.
- Facilitate community-led monitoring using scorecards, satisfaction surveys, observation checklists, and spot checks.
- Analyse data with communities in accessible formats to identify gaps and agree on actions.
- Link community monitoring to subnational/national systems.
- Transition monitoring responsibilities to local committees (WASH committees, mother care groups).
- Facilitate community-to-community learning exchanges and peer networks.

2.4.1.4 Utilizing monitoring data

Translate data into evidence-based decisions and accountability.

- Analyse findings to assess reach, quality, and equity; identify barriers; recommend improvements.

- Develop user-friendly dashboards, infographics, and reports for diverse stakeholders.
- Convene periodic data review meetings with communities, the government, and partners for course corrections.
- Document and disseminate promising practices through knowledge products and learning events.
- Monitor safety, privacy, cultural acceptability, and accessibility of facilities (especially for women, children, and persons with disabilities).
- Develop policy briefs and advocacy materials to influence WASH-nutrition policies, budgets, and resource allocation.

2.4.2 Key monitoring indicators

Monitoring integrated WASH and nutrition programming requires a combination of output, outcome, and process indicators. Key indicators include the following.

WASH and nutrition outcomes:

- Child stunting, wasting, and underweight prevalence.
- Minimum acceptable diet (children aged 6–23 months).
- Diarrhea/enteric infection prevalence (under five).
- Sufficiency of caregiver's time for child care.

WASH access and practices:

- Household access to basic WASH facilities.
- Safe water storage/treatment practices.
- Handwashing facilities with soap and water.
- Safe disposal of child feces.
- Mother–child dyads practising key hygiene behaviours.
- Water point functionality and distance (less than a 30-minute round trip).
- Communities maintaining criteria for open defecation-free status.
- Caregiver knows how to prepare oral rehydration salts.
- Safe food preparation/storage practices.

Service performance and capacity:

- WASH facilities in health/nutrition centres meeting minimum standards.

- Community health/nutrition workers trained on integrated WASH-nutrition.
- The functionality of community WASH-nutrition management committees.

2.4.3 Monitoring methods and tools

- Household surveys (knowledge, attitude, and practice (KAP), diarrhea prevalence).
- Health facility assessments (WASH FIT, records review).
- Community assessments (participatory mapping, focus group discussions).
- Programme reports/coverage data.
- Observation checklists (handwashing, food hygiene, feeding demonstrations).

2.4.4 Monitoring roles and responsibilities

Actor	*Responsibilities*
Community	Participate in assessments, collect/analyse data, develop action plans, provide feedback, transition to local committees.
Implementing agencies	Coordinate harmonized systems, train staff, compile/analyse data, facilitate evidence-based planning.
Government	Oversee national/subnational monitoring, integrate indicators into sectoral systems, convene reviews, inform policy.

2.4.5 Monitoring timeline and deliverables

- *Monthly*: facility/community monitoring visits and data collection.
- *Quarterly*: data compilation and dashboards.
- *Biannually*: community assessments; data review/action planning workshops; knowledge products.
- *Annually*: sector performance review and planning.

Key deliverables:

- Integrated M&E framework and indicators.
- Assessment reports (baseline, midline, endline).
- Dashboards and infographics.
- Data review meeting minutes with action points.
- Community scorecards and monitoring reports.
- Case studies, learning briefs, policy briefs.

CHAPTER 3

Brief 3. Integration in emergencies

Guideline for coordinating WASH with health at the community level

Source document: Chapter 4 in Sorensen, Nikolas, Mariëlle Snel, James Ray III, and Syed Yasir Ahmad Khan. 2026. *Building Resilience: Coordination Guidelines for Integrated WASH, Health, and Nutrition Programming in Crisis Settings*. Practical Action Publishing. http://doi.org/10.3362/9781788534710

3.1 Executive summary

This guideline provides essential guidance on coordination for community-level implementers overseeing WASH and health initiatives during emergencies. It supports a rapid response while emphasizing long-term resilience, serving as one of four complementary guidelines designed as an integrated framework for WASH coordination with health and nutrition at both national and community levels. This guideline was developed by the WASH Road Map in consultation with numerous other professionals.

3.1.1 Purpose

This guideline helps frontline workers, community leaders, and local organizations integrate WASH and health interventions during emergencies through structured, time-bound actions. It provides a people-centred approach for rapidly improving WASH services in health facilities and communities, while strengthening local stakeholder capacity to sustain these services in the long term. It upholds the rights outlined in the Humanitarian Charter and aligns with global commitments to advance universal health coverage and primary healthcare.

3.1.2 Key actions

Actions	*WASH*	*Health*	*Timeframe*	*Guideline sections*	*Practitioners' Toolkit sections*
Activate health facility-led coordination platform	Identify WASH representatives and align with health facility priorities	Lead the coordination platform with senior facility management and support from local government	Within 48 hours	3.2.4	1.1, 1.2, 1.5
Conduct rapid community and facility assessments	Assess WASH conditions in communities and health facilities; map stakeholders and capacities	Provide input on health risks and priorities; assess health facility WASH conditions	Days 1–10	3.2.5, 3.2.6, 3.3.1.1	1.3, 2.1, 2.2, 2.4, 2.6, 3.4, 3.5
Implement priority WASH interventions and behaviour change	Provide WASH interventions; promote critical hygiene behaviours	Provide guidance on health-related WASH priorities; support hygiene promotion in health settings	Days 1–14	3.3.1.2, 3.3.1.3	4.4, 4.5, 2.4
Develop localized action plans and establish partnerships	Align WASH activities with health programme objectives; engage community leaders in WASH planning	Incorporate WASH messages into health programmes; establish strategic partnerships with development actors	Days 5–21	3.2.7, 3.2.6, 3.3.1.6	3.1, 3.2, 3.3, 3.7, 4.1
Strengthen local governance and establish monitoring systems	Build capacity of local WASH committees; set up referral pathways between WASH and health services	Build the capacity of community health workers; establish accountability and information-sharing systems	Days 10–30	3.2.8, 3.2.11, 3.3.1.4, 3.3.1.5	3.4, 3.6, 4.2, 5.1, 5.2, 5.3, 5.4

(*Continues*)

(Continued)

Actions	*WASH*	*Health*	*Timeframe*	*Guideline sections*	*Practitioners' Toolkit sections*
Establish facility-based WASH improvement teams and secure high-level support	Support WASH assessments and improvements in health facilities; align with national standards	Oversee facility WASH improvements; engage senior ministry leadership for resource commitments	Days 7–30	3.2.9, 3.2.10	2.4, 2.5, 2.6, 4.5
Develop sustainable systems and market solutions	Build local WASH market systems; support community-managed WASH services transition	Integrate WASH into health system strengthening; support health facility sustainability planning	Days 30–90	3.2.12, 3.3.2.1, 3.3.2.2, 3.3.2.4	3.3, 3.4, 4.8, 4.9
Facilitate learning and establish resilience measures	Capture community perspectives on WASH improvements; document innovations and adaptations	Document health facility WASH improvements; establish emergency preparedness systems	Days 45–90	3.3.2.3, 3.2.12	5.5, 5.6, 4.7, 4.9

3.1.3 Framework pillars

Five pillars guide health facility WASH improvement:

1. *Community engagement*: Involve health facility staff, community representatives, and local partners as active participants throughout WASH improvement.
2. *Local assessment*: Assess WASH infrastructure, practices, and skills at facility and community levels to identify critical gaps.
3. *Coordinated implementation*: Upgrade WASH services, change behaviours, and establish a culture of hygiene and safety.
4. *Local capacity building*: Build the capacity of health workers and community partners to operate and maintain the WASH infrastructure.
5. *Community monitoring*: Support facilities and communities in establishing systems for ongoing data collection, review, and quality improvement.

This guideline integrates climate resilience, protection, gender equity, and social inclusion while clarifying roles across government, humanitarian, and community actors. It bridges emergency response and long-term development at the national level.

3.2 Stakeholder coordination

Effective coordination of WASH and health interventions at the community level requires engagement of a diverse range of local stakeholders who directly interface with families and individuals. This guideline section outlines the approach to stakeholder coordination with special emphasis on health facilities as focal points for integrated WASH and health interventions and community outreach. This approach recognizes that sustainable improvements in health outcomes require collaborative efforts between clinical care providers and environmental health practitioners.

3.2.1 Stakeholder identification checklist

The seven key stakeholder categories essential for effective community WASH and health coordination:

1. government authorities
2. humanitarian and development organizations
3. community representatives

4. the private sector
5. academic and research institutions
6. UN agencies and donors
7. inter-cluster coordination

3.2.2 Strengthening meaningful participation

For effective community WASH and health coordination, leadership roles and decision-making authority should be allocated to health facility staff, community representatives, and local officials to prevent external agency domination. The coordination platform should actively reduce participation barriers for marginalized populations by adopting inclusive meeting practices, providing accessible information formats, and offering leadership opportunities, with dedicated seats for representatives of vulnerable groups. Developing sustained partnerships with local academic and training institutes helps produce evidence, build capacity, and expand effective practices at the community level. Collaboration with trusted male and female community leaders, including informal leaders such as elders, is crucial for facilitating programme entry, building trust, and shifting WASH and health behaviour norms. The coordination mechanism should focus on building local teams' capacity to effectively engage stakeholders, lead multisectoral initiatives, and make evidence-based decisions. Social accountability mechanisms, such as community scorecards and participatory monitoring, empower communities to hold health facilities accountable for service quality and sustainability. Community dialogues and self-help initiatives foster local ownership. At the same time, the joint engagement of medical and administrative staff in planning activities creates a shared sense of ownership over WASH health improvements in facilities and surrounding communities.

3.2.3 Coordination mechanisms

Critical action summary

Critical action	*Timeframe*	*Lead responsibility*
Activate health facility-led coordination platform	Within 48 hours	Senior facility management
Map and engage local stakeholder structures	By day 5	Platform leadership team

(*Continues*)

(Continued)

Critical action	*Timeframe*	*Lead responsibility*
Establish strategic partnerships with development actors	By day 7	Platform coordination team
Develop localized multisectoral action plans	By day 14	Platform with community input
Establish accountability and information-sharing systems	By day 10	Platform-monitoring team
Form facility-based WASH improvement teams	By day 7	Facility management

3.2.4 Coordination platform activation

Action: Establish an inclusive health facility-led WASH coordination platform within 48 hours

Lead: Senior facility management with support from local government and partners

Key steps:

- Activate the platform with representatives from key departments, the local government, civil society, and the community.
- Define clear roles, responsibilities, and accountability mechanisms.
- Hold regular meetings to assess needs, set priorities, and track progress; share minutes for transparency.

Representation: Ensure leadership roles and dedicated seats for women, youth, marginalized groups, and WASH/health technical experts.

Context adaptations

Low-resource settings	*Fragile contexts*	*Resource constraints*
Simplified structures (three to five representatives); visual/verbal over written; leverage informal networks; focus on one to two essential actions	Flexible/mobile delivery over fixed infrastructure; rapid communication via radio/mobile; work through neutral actors; plan for service continuity	Low-cost local materials; peer-to-peer volunteer training; graduated cost sharing; prioritize behaviour change interventions

3.2.5 Local stakeholder engagement

Action: Map and engage existing local structures and stakeholder groups

Lead: Platform leadership team with community mobilization specialists

Key structures to engage:

- *Governance*: development committees, local governance bodies.
- *Health*: management teams, health committees, community health worker networks.
- *WASH*: committees, water user associations.
- *Community*: women's groups, youth organizations, religious/traditional leaders, school committees.

Decentralization strategies:

- Establish WASH subcommittees at the village/catchment level with clear mandates.
- Link local committees to the facility platform and national mechanisms.
- Assign leadership roles to community representatives and build their decision-making capacity.

Implementation steps:

- Map existing structures and assess their capacity/representation.
- Develop a tailored engagement strategy for each stakeholder group.
- Establish a two-way information flow and provide role orientation.
- Schedule regular cross-level coordination.

3.2.6 Strategic partnerships

Action: Establish strategic partnerships with development actors

Lead: Platform coordination team with support from facility management

Key partners: NGOs/civil society, UN agencies, private sector, academic/research institutions, technical resource partners.

Partnership development:

- Identify partners with relevant expertise and resources.
- Define supporting roles that complement (not undermine) local leadership.
- Formalize through MOUs with clear transition plans for external support.

MOU components:

- Roles, responsibilities, and resource commitments.
- Information sharing and decision-making protocols.
- Sustainability, transition, and accountability mechanisms.

3.2.7 Localized action planning

Action: Develop localized, multisectoral WASH and health action plans

Lead: Platform coordination team with community input and technical guidance

Planning process:

- Base plans on facility assessments and community input.
- Integrate WASH into broader health/development plans.
- Leverage multisectoral collaboration and pooled resources.

Plan components:

- Situation analysis, priority issues, and risk management strategies.
- Objectives, measurable targets, and M&E framework.
- Activities with timelines, responsible parties, and resource/funding sources.
- Capacity-building needs and approaches.

Implementation requirements:

- Define clear roles; emphasize local ownership and capacity development.
- Mobilize partners to address capacity gaps.
- Disseminate widely in accessible formats/languages; use as an advocacy tool for political and financial support.

3.2.8 Accountability and information sharing

Action: Strengthen accountability, transparency, and information-sharing systems

Lead: Platform-monitoring team with support from information management specialists

Accountability mechanisms:

- Establish clear targets/indicators integrated into existing monitoring systems.
- Agree on common data definitions, collection methodologies, and sharing protocols.
- Schedule periodic coordination meetings; ensure transparent financial reporting.

Feedback system requirements:

- Safe, accessible, context-appropriate grievance channels (multiple formats for varying literacy levels).
- Clear investigation/resolution processes with regular communication on actions taken.
- Confidentiality protections; document and analyse feedback trends.

Information management:

- Designate focal points at all levels with regular reporting timelines and standardized tools.
- Develop visualization tools; build capacity for data collection and analysis.
- Use information products to influence decision-making.
- Committees supervise activities, mobilize resources, and inform partners at their respective levels.

3.2.9 Facility-based WASH improvement

Action: Establish facility-based WASH improvement teams

Lead: Facility management with support from WASH technical specialists

Team composition:

- Dedicated clean clinic teams with staff from clinical, support, and administrative departments.
- Community liaisons, patient representatives, and technical advisers as needed.

Team responsibilities:

- Lead facility WASH assessments; develop and implement improvement plans.
- Monitor and maintain WASH infrastructure and practices.
- Train staff on WASH protocols; engage patients/communities in improvements.
- Document and share learning and best practices.

Implementation steps:

1. Appoint team members with clear terms of reference; provide orientation/training.
2. Conduct a baseline assessment of facility WASH conditions.
3. Develop a prioritized improvement plan with clear targets.
4. Implement regular monitoring, maintenance, meetings, and reporting.

3.2.10 High-level support and buy-in

Action: Secure high-level institutional support for WASH and health coordination

Lead: Platform leadership with support from senior health officials

Key steps:

- Conduct an initial WASH evaluation in health facilities; present the results to senior Ministry of Health leadership.
- Secure endorsement and resource commitments from authorities.
- Engage facility directors and district health authorities; build ownership of WASH improvements.
- Host stakeholder workshops so they can familiarize themselves with the assessment tools.

Advocacy strategies:

- Link WASH to health outcome priorities; highlight disease reduction potential and cost-effectiveness of integrated approaches.
- Demonstrate alignment with national health priorities.
- Use visual documentation and success stories from other locations.

3.2.11 Monitoring systems and learning

Action: Establish robust monitoring systems and feedback loops

Lead: Platform-monitoring team with support from district health officers

Key monitoring elements:

- Adherence to standard operating procedures for WASH and IPC; infrastructure functionality and maintenance.
- Staff knowledge/practice of WASH standards; disease surveillance and outbreak detection.
- Community engagement, satisfaction, and sustainability of improvements.

Supportive supervision approach:

- Regular supportive supervision by trained district officers with joint multi-stakeholder monitoring visits.
- Emphasis on improvement over inspection; peer-to-peer learning and on-the-job coaching.
- Document and share good practices.

Learning and adaptation:

- Hold regular review/reflection meetings; document lessons learned and challenges.
- Adapt approaches based on monitoring data; share experiences across facilities and communities.
- Continuous staff development and skill building.

3.2.12 Sustainability and resilience

Action: Promote sustainability, learning, and resilience

Lead: Platform leadership with facility management and local authorities

Resource sustainability:

- Determine long-term WASH infrastructure resource needs; identify sustainable funding sources.
- Advocate for integration in facility/district budgets; explore pooled resource options across facilities and sectors.
- Develop innovative financing mechanisms.

Capacity building for sustainability:

- Continuously build staff and community capacity; promote local innovation to reduce external dependence.
- Identify and mentor WASH champions; create peer-support networks for knowledge sharing.
- Develop locally appropriate maintenance systems and supply chains.

Resilience building:

- Document and share lessons learned; participate in learning exchanges at various levels.
- Integrate emergency preparedness in WASH planning; build the local capacity for a rapid response.
- Consider climate change and environmental sustainability.
- National committees should conduct regular strategy implementation reviews to identify areas for improvement.

3.3 Emergency WASH actions

This section outlines the critical WASH interventions needed in the acute phase of an emergency to rapidly address public health risks and prevent the spread of disease. It covers key aspects of emergency WASH response, including rapid assessments, prioritized interventions, hygiene promotion, local governance capacity strengthening, disease risk mitigation, and community-driven planning. The section emphasizes the importance of community engagement, participatory methods, and multisectoral coordination to ensure that WASH actions are relevant, acceptable, and effective in meeting the immediate needs of affected populations.

3.3.1 Emergency actions (days 0–14)

The emergency actions phase focuses on quickly identifying and addressing the most pressing WASH needs in collaboration with affected communities. It involves rapid assessments to understand the local context, capacities, and priorities, followed by the implementation of priority interventions to reduce public health risks. Key activities include ensuring access to safe water, providing appropriate sanitation facilities, distributing essential hygiene items, and promoting critical hygiene behaviours.

3.3.1.1 Rapidly assess WASH with communities

Timing: Initiate within 72 hours; complete within 14 days with regular updates as the situation evolves.

Key steps:

1. Mobilize community leaders, health workers, and volunteers to jointly assess WASH conditions, practices, and local resources, using participatory methods (transect walks, focus groups, community mapping).
2. Prioritize high-risk households and vulnerable groups (e.g. undernourished children, limited WASH access) to identify critical gaps and inform response targeting.
3. Engage diverse community members – particularly women, youth, and marginalized groups – to understand specific WASH needs and priorities.
4. Analyse findings with community representatives to co-develop inclusive local WASH improvement plans responsive to women, children, elderly people, and persons with disabilities.
5. Identify and engage local influencers to champion behaviour change and promote community ownership.
6. Conduct comprehensive health facility WASH assessments across infrastructure, supplies, practices, and protocols to identify priority improvements.

3.3.1.2 Implement prioritized WASH interventions

Timing: Begin priority interventions within 72 hours of initial assessments; progressively expand coverage and quality based on evolving needs and capacities.

Key steps:

1. Work with community leaders and WASH committees to select and implement quick-impact interventions, addressing pressing risks (e.g. household water treatment, emergency latrines, public handwashing stations).
2. Mobilize local resources, skills, and capacities; engage community members to contribute labour, materials, and ideas while providing tools, technical guidance, and skill building.
3. Distribute essential WASH supplies (soap, water containers, menstrual hygiene products) to the most vulnerable households; pair with culturally appropriate demonstrations on proper use and critical hygiene behaviours.
4. Monitor interventions through community feedback, spot checks, and simple indicators (e.g. latrine usage, handwashing station functionality); adapt based on data and input.
5. Prioritize critical health facility WASH actions: functional hand hygiene stations at points of care, medical device decontamination, healthcare waste management, and environmental cleaning.
6. Rapidly repair existing water/sanitation systems or deploy temporary solutions (water trucking, treatment kits, storage); transition to durable, locally manageable options as soon as feasible.

3.3.1.3 Promote participatory hygiene behaviour change

Timing: Launch within the first 14 days using assessment data to prioritize target behaviours and audiences; intensify and adapt based on community feedback and disease surveillance data.

Key steps:

1. Engage community members to design context-specific hygiene campaigns; train trusted local influencers (community health workers, teachers, religious leaders) to model and promote key behaviours.

2. Develop targeted hygiene messages tailored for pregnant women, young children, elderly people, persons with disabilities, and those with chronic illness; focus on WASH practices preventing diarrhea and respiratory infections.
3. Support community volunteers to establish community-led monitoring using simple indicators (e.g. household soap availability, observed handwashing at critical times); provide regular feedback to adapt strategies.
4. Integrate hygiene promotion into existing community platforms (care groups, savings associations, schools) to maximize reach across multiple touchpoints.
5. Engage health facility staff and community health workers in participatory sessions to identify target hygiene behaviours; co-design facility-based behaviour change strategies leveraging existing IPC protocols.

3.3.1.4 Strengthen local WASH governance capacities

Timing: Within the first 30 days, establish or reactivate representative WASH committees; provide ongoing capacity building throughout the emergency, recovery, and development phases.

Key steps:

1. Work with local leaders to establish/reactivate community WASH committees with diverse representation (women, youth, marginalized groups); develop clear roles, responsibilities, and action plans.
2. Provide hands-on training and mentoring in participatory planning, problem solving, resource mobilization, and monitoring; use adult learning techniques (demonstrations, role-plays, peer exchange).
3. Connect WASH committees with local government and nutrition partners to advocate for WASH prioritization in emergency response plans and funding; facilitate joint planning and coordination.
4. Facilitate community-led asset mapping to identify existing WASH resources, service providers, and local influencers; encourage documentation and sharing of lessons learned (storytelling, photos, videos) for peer learning.

5. Strengthen health facility management team capacity to lead and sustain WASH improvements through training and support in assessment, action planning, resource mobilization, and monitoring; encourage peer learning among facilities.

3.3.1.5 Assess and mitigate WASH-related disease risks

Timing: Initial risk assessments within 14 days, updated regularly based on surveillance and community feedback; priority mitigation measures within 30 days.

Key steps:

1. Collaborate with community health workers and local health facilities to identify and track households at high risk of WASH-related diseases, particularly children with severe acute malnutrition.
2. Coordinate with nutrition actors to ensure high-risk households receive targeted WASH interventions (hygiene promotion, water treatment, improved sanitation); jointly develop criteria and referral protocols.
3. Establish community-based referral systems between WASH, health, and nutrition services; train community health workers on referral processes and counter-referral tracking; ensure caregivers of undernourished children receive hygiene kits and WASH information during treatment.
4. Support oral rehydration therapy points, handwashing stations, and safe play spaces at nutrition treatment sites; provide WASH training and supplies to nutrition staff and volunteers.
5. Strengthen health facility disease surveillance for rapid outbreak detection and response; establish clear reporting protocols and train staff on early warning signs and outbreak control.

3.3.1.6 Make community-driven WASH improvement plans

Timing: Initiate participatory planning within the first 30 days; update and adapt plans regularly based on monitoring data and community feedback.

Key steps:

1. Facilitate participatory planning sessions where community members jointly analyse WASH challenges, identify solutions, and develop context-specific improvement plans.
2. Prioritize low-cost, feasible interventions, leveraging local knowledge, skills, and resources; encourage incremental, achievable actions rather than waiting for external assistance.
3. Identify capacity gaps and deliver tailored, hands-on development through local trainers and peer-to-peer learning; partner with local vocational institutes and universities.
4. Align emergency WASH plans with broader community development goals and sustainability considerations; work with health, education, and nutrition partners to embed WASH across sectors.
5. Advocate for inclusion of community WASH priorities in local government recovery/development plans; support health facilities to develop improvement plans progressively, meeting national standards.

3.3.2 Resilience actions (days 14–90)

As the emergency response progresses, it is critical to focus on integrating WASH and health interventions with local capacities and systems to ensure their sustainability and long-term impact. Key aspects of this integration process include strengthening local WASH governance structures, building the capacity of local actors to manage and maintain WASH services, promoting sustainable behaviour change, and developing market-based solutions for WASH products and services. By investing in local capacities and systems, responders can help build the foundation for a more resilient and locally led WASH sector.

3.3.2.1 Develop sustainable community WASH governance

Timing: Ongoing support to community WASH committees throughout the emergency, recovery, and development phases, progressively building autonomy and sustainability.

Key steps:

1. Provide ongoing coaching and organizational development; facilitate visioning and strategic planning for long-term goals and sustainability.
2. Establish clear by-laws, leadership transition processes, and financial transparency mechanisms; ensure committees track infrastructure functionality, service access, and equity of use.
3. Develop community-led monitoring systems using participatory tools; establish feedback loops where data informs regular action-planning meetings.
4. Strengthen peer-to-peer learning networks through cross-community exchanges, competitions, and storytelling events.
5. Establish knowledge management systems to document, share, and scale up best practices and innovations.
6. Engage municipal authorities for ongoing support of health facility WASH infrastructure; establish clear roles and coordination mechanisms between facilities and local government WASH departments.

3.3.2.2 Strengthen local WASH market systems

Timing: Initial market assessments within the first 30 days; continuously strengthen local WASH markets throughout the emergency, recovery, and development phases.

Key steps:

1. Conduct market assessments to identify constraints and opportunities in local WASH supply chains, including the availability, quality, and affordability of essential products/services.
2. Provide business coaching, training, and market linkages to WASH enterprises; prioritize women and youth-led businesses; facilitate financing access through savings groups, microfinance, and grants.
3. Partner with WASH committees to design and pilot market-based models for sustainable services (e.g. sanitation enterprises, water kiosks); use community feedback to refine.
4. Work with local authorities to strengthen the policy and regulatory environment for WASH enterprises, supporting service expansion and consumer protection.

5. Address health facility WASH supply chain bottlenecks; improve the availability, quality, and affordability of commodities; establish facility-level procurement and inventory management systems.
6. Train local personnel on water quality monitoring, system operation and maintenance (O&M), and supply chain management; progressively transfer skills and responsibilities to local actors.

3.3.2.3 Facilitate participatory learning and adaptation

Timing: Establish participatory learning and adaptation mechanisms within the first 90 days; maintain and strengthen throughout the emergency, recovery, and development phases.

Key steps:

1. Establish community-led learning platforms using participatory tools to analyse monitoring data, document lessons, and adjust strategies.
2. Support knowledge capture and sharing through diverse media (storytelling, videos, radio, community theatre) to disseminate good practices.
3. Synthesize learnings into simple, action-oriented materials; distribute through community meetings, local media, and stakeholder forums.
4. Organize periodic multi-stakeholder review meetings with community representatives, local authorities, and partners; use community-generated evidence to inform sector planning and advocacy.
5. Facilitate participatory action research and learning exchanges within/among health facilities; support staff to document experiences through case studies, learning briefs, and presentations.

3.3.2.4 Transition to local systems for sustainable services

Timing: Develop transition plans with local stakeholders within the first year; use a phased approach, gradually transferring roles, responsibilities, and resources over a multi-year period.

Key steps:

1. Assess the capacity of local governments, utilities, and service providers to assume long-term WASH management; identify gaps and develop joint capacity-building plans.
2. Facilitate dialogue between WASH committees, local authorities, and service providers to formalize transition plans through MOUs; clarify roles, responsibilities, resources, and a phased handover timeline.
3. Provide technical assistance to local authorities in planning, budgeting, performance monitoring, and customer engagement; prioritize skills transfer for sustained management.
4. Integrate emergency WASH infrastructure into local systems with adequate O&M provisions; align with national policies and standards; avoid abrupt handovers, risking service disruptions.
5. Establish dedicated WASH focal points within the local government with clear job descriptions, targets, and reporting lines; provide ongoing mentoring and peer support.
6. Monitor the transition using agreed performance metrics and milestones; provide backstopping and technical assistance to ensure service continuity and quality.

3.4 Monitoring

3.4.1 Key monitoring activities

3.4.1.1 Engaging communities

Participatory monitoring by community members is critical for local ownership and data relevance. Affected people should be central to deciding what to measure and how to act on findings.

- Consult diverse community groups to define context-specific WASH/health monitoring priorities and indicators.
- Establish inclusive monitoring teams, with women, youth, and marginalized groups in lead roles; train monitors to collect, analyse, and communicate data using participatory tools.
- Facilitate community validation of results to inform local action and advocacy.
- Conduct quarterly community meetings to review findings, identify bottlenecks, and co-develop action plans using visual tools (scorecards, maps).

3.4.1.2 Harmonizing indicators and systems

Community-level indicators should harmonize with national systems while reflecting local realities.

- Develop core community WASH/health indicators, integrating with national frameworks (SDGs, WHO/UNICEF JMP definitions).
- Disaggregate all data by gender, age, disability, and vulnerability.
- Standardize data collection tools, methods, and reporting formats across community to national levels.
- Establish data sharing protocols between community, health-facility, and government systems; use digital platforms where feasible.

3.4.1.3 Strengthening community capacities

Build local capacities through learning by doing, peer exchange, and integration with wider processes.

- Build on existing community structures for participatory planning and monitoring.
- Develop simple, visual monitoring tools adapted to local needs, languages, and literacies.
- Provide hands-on training for community monitors on data collection, management, analysis, and use.
- Facilitate community-to-community learning through exchange visits and joint events; establish peer mentoring and refresher sessions.

3.4.1.4 Utilizing monitoring data

Monitoring data should inform real-time decision-making at all levels through user-friendly formats and effective feedback loops.

- Analyse data to assess progress, equity, and effectiveness; produce accessible reports, dashboards, and scorecards.
- Convene participatory forums for community representatives, health workers, and authorities to review results and agree on actions.

- Use data to inform social accountability efforts (participatory budgeting, community scorecards, citizen report cards).
- Advocate for community-monitoring evidence to inform higher-level policies, plans, and budgets.
- Establish safe, accessible grievance redress mechanisms with transparent follow-up.

3.4.2 Key monitoring indicators

Domain	*Indicators*
Access and use	Household access to basic water/sanitation; households with handwashing facilities (soap/water); knowledge/practice of key hygiene behaviours; safe water handling/storage; safe fecal waste management; proximity to improved water source (≤500m)
Functionality and quality	Water point functionality; sanitation facility condition (clean, private, maintained); health facility WASH services; water quality (turbidity <5 NTU, chlorine 0.5–1.0 mg/L); daily water availability (min 20L/person); latrine ratios (≤20 communal, ≤50 public)
Governance and sustainability	Active WASH/health committees with inclusive membership; up-to-date management/maintenance plans; user fee collection and transparent financial management; facilities meeting national standards
Health outcomes	WASH-related disease prevalence (especially under-five diarrhea); child stunting/wasting; outbreak detection and response within 48 hours

3.4.3 Monitoring methods and tools

- *Community level*: WASH mapping, transect walks, observation checklists, participatory scorecards, social audits.
- *Household level*: surveys/interviews on KAP; structured observations of handwashing, latrine use, and waste disposal.
- *Health facility level*: sanitary inspections, water quality testing, IPC audits, and assessments of PPE, cleaning protocols, waste segregation, and supplies.

3.4.4 Monitoring roles and responsibilities

Actor	*Key responsibilities*
Community	Identify priorities/indicators; collect and report data; analyse results and develop action plans; provide feedback to service providers; participate in multi-stakeholder forums
Implementing agencies	Co-design participatory monitoring systems; train and mentor monitors; conduct supervision visits; facilitate community–facility dialogue; aggregate data for sectoral processes
Government	Coordinate community-based monitoring within national systems; integrate data into national databases; convene joint review meetings; allocate resources; utilize evidence for policy

3.4.5 Monitoring timeline and deliverables

Frequency	*Activity*
Acute phase	Rapid WASH/health assessments (updated quarterly)
Monthly	Monitoring visits and data collection
Bi-monthly	Community review meetings
Quarterly	Reports to subnational coordination
Annual	Participatory evaluations of monitoring systems

Key deliverables:

- Monitoring framework, manual, tools, and training pack.
- Database and dashboard for all sites.
- Quarterly bulletins and scorecards.
- Biannual reports on system functionality and data quality.
- Learning briefs and multimedia products.
- Policy recommendations for institutionalizing community-led monitoring.

CHAPTER 4

Brief 4. Integration in emergencies

Guideline for coordinating WASH with nutrition at the community level

Source document: Chapter 5 in Sorensen, Nikolas, Mariëlle Snel, James Ray III, and Syed Yasir Ahmad Khan. 2026. *Building Resilience: Coordination Guidelines for Integrated WASH, Health, and Nutrition Programming in Crisis Settings*. Practical Action Publishing. http://doi.org/10.3362/9781788534710

4.1 Executive summary

This guideline provides essential guidance on coordination for community-level implementers overseeing WASH and nutrition initiatives during emergencies. It supports a rapid response while emphasizing long-term resilience, serving as one of four complementary guidelines designed as an integrated framework for WASH coordination with health and nutrition at both national and community levels. This guideline was developed by the WASH Road Map in consultation with numerous other professionals.

4.1.1 Purpose

This guideline helps frontline workers, community leaders, and local organizations integrate WASH and nutrition interventions during emergencies through structured, time-bound actions. It operationalizes a multisectoral approach to address the underlying causes of undernutrition at the household and individual level, particularly during the critical first 1,000 days from conception to a child's second birthday. It upholds the rights outlined in the Humanitarian Charter and aligns with global commitments to advance universal health coverage and primary healthcare.

4.1.2 Key actions

Actions	*WASH*	*Nutrition*	*Timeframe*	*Guideline sections*	*Practitioners' Toolkit sections*
Establish community WASH-nutrition committee	Identify WASH representatives and engage community leaders	Identify nutrition representatives and engage community health workers	Within 1 week	4.2.4	1.1, 1.2, 4.8
Conduct participatory community assessment and map existing structures	Assess WASH conditions, practices, and capacities; map WASH-related community structures	Assess nutrition status, practices, and capacities; map nutrition-related community networks	Days 3–10	4.2.5, 4.2.6, 4.3.1.1	1.3, 1.4, 2.1, 2.2, 2.3, 3.4
Implement minimum WASH package and integrate with nutrition programmes	Provide WASH interventions tailored to nutrition needs; align with nutrition programme objectives	Incorporate WASH messages and activities into nutrition programmes; provide guidance on nutrition-sensitive WASH priorities	Days 1–14	4.3.1.2, 4.3.1.3	2.1, 2.2, 2.3, 4.4, 4.6, 4.10
Develop joint strategies and engage community actors	Contribute WASH expertise to integrated strategy development; involve community members in WASH intervention design	Contribute nutrition expertise to integrated strategy development; involve community members in promoting nutrition-sensitive WASH practices	Days 7–21	4.2.7, 4.3.1.4	3.1, 3.2, 3.3, 4.1, 4.7

(*Continues*)

(Continued)

Actions	*WASH*	*Nutrition*	*Timeframe*	*Guideline sections*	*Practitioners' Toolkit sections*
Establish communication mechanisms and school-based integration	Set up communication and referral pathways between WASH and nutrition services; promote WASH in schools integrated with nutrition education	Set up communication pathways between nutrition and WASH services; promote nutrition education in schools integrated with WASH	Days 10–30	4.2.8, 4.2.9, 4.3.2.3	4.3, 4.7, 5.2, 5.3
Strengthen local capacity and align with national systems	Build capacity of local WASH committees; ensure community-level WASH interventions adhere to national standards	Build capacity of community nutrition volunteers; ensure community nutrition interventions align with national strategies	Days 30–90	4.3.2.1, 4.3.2.3	3.4, 3.6, 4.2, 4.8, 4.9
Support innovations and promote nutrition-sensitive programming	Document local WASH innovations; promote nutrition-sensitive WASH programming approaches	Document local nutrition innovations; integrate nutrition considerations into WASH strategies throughout response	Days 30–90	4.3.2.4, 4.3.2.6	3.2, 4.4, 5.5
Establish monitoring systems and plan transition	Collect and respond to community feedback on WASH interventions; transition ownership to community structures	Collect and respond to community feedback on nutrition interventions; transition ownership to local structures	Days 14–90	4.2.10, 4.2.11, 4.3.2.5, 4.4	5.1, 5.3, 5.5, 5.6, 3.4

4.1.3 Framework pillars

Five pillars guide WASH-nutrition integration:

1. *Community engagement*: Partner with communities throughout intervention design, implementation, and monitoring.
2. *Local assessment*: Identify WASH-related nutrition risks and vulnerable household groups.
3. *Coordinated implementation*: Prioritize actions linking improved WASH to better nutrition outcomes.
4. *Local capacity building*: Strengthen skills of health workers, caregivers, and local structures for sustained interventions.
5. *Community monitoring*: Establish systems to track outcomes and drive continuous improvement.

This guideline integrates climate resilience, protection, gender equity, and social inclusion while clarifying roles across government, humanitarian, and community actors. It bridges emergency response and long-term development at the national level.

4.2 Stakeholder coordination

Community-level coordination of WASH and nutrition interventions depends on the active engagement of local stakeholders and institutions. This guideline section emphasizes the importance of local ownership and contextual understanding in stakeholder coordination. Effective community-level coordination bridges the gap between national policies and household practices, ensuring that interventions are culturally appropriate, accessible, and sustainable within local contexts.

4.2.1 Stakeholder identification checklist

The seven key stakeholder categories that should be involved in the community-level WASH and nutrition multi-stakeholder platform:

- local government authorities
- community-based organizations and civil society
- health and nutrition service providers
- WASH service providers and the private sector
- schools and educational institutions and camp coordination actors

- local media and communication channels
- humanitarian and development partners

4.2.2 Strengthening meaningful participation

At the community level, strengthening WASH and nutrition coordination requires allocating leadership roles and decision-making authority to community representatives and local officials while preventing external agency domination. Coordination teams should actively reduce participation barriers for marginalized populations through inclusive meetings, accessible information formats, and dedicated leadership opportunities. Sustained partnerships with local academic and training institutes are valuable for producing contextually relevant evidence, building local capacity, and expanding effective practices. Collaboration with trusted male and female community leaders and influencers, including informal leaders such as elders, is essential to facilitate programme entry, build community trust, and shift WASH and nutrition behaviour norms. The coordination platform should invest in building the capacity of local teams to effectively engage stakeholders, lead multisectoral initiatives, and make evidence-based decisions. Employing social accountability mechanisms, such as community scorecards and participatory monitoring, empowers communities to monitor WASH and nutrition service quality, while community dialogues and self-help initiatives foster local ownership and the sustainability of integrated interventions.

4.2.3 Coordination mechanisms

Critical action summary

Critical action	*Timeframe*	*Lead responsibility*
Establish community WASH-nutrition committee	Within the first week	Community leader with WASH/nutrition sector support
Conduct participatory community mapping	By day 10	Committee with technical support
Map existing community platforms and networks	By day 14	Committee with community leaders
Develop joint WASH-nutrition strategies	By day 21	Committee with technical advisers

(*Continues*)

(Continued)

Critical action	*Timeframe*	*Lead responsibility*
Establish two-way communication mechanisms	By day 14	Committee with communication specialists
Engage schools as integration entry points	By week 3	Committee with education partners

4.2.4 Establishing a community coordination committee

Action: Establish an inclusive community WASH and nutrition committee within the first week

Lead: Community leader with WASH and nutrition sector representatives

Key steps:

- Set up a committee with co-leadership between community leaders and sector representatives.
- Include representatives from all key stakeholder groups.
- Develop terms of reference with clear roles, decision-making processes, and a regular meeting schedule.

Context adaptations

Low-resource settings	*Fragile contexts*	*Resource constraints*
Simplified structures (three to five reps); visual/verbal over written; leverage informal networks; focus on one to two essential actions	Flexible/mobile delivery over fixed infrastructure; rapid communication via radio/mobile; work through neutral actors; plan for service continuity	Low-cost local materials; peer-to-peer volunteer training; graduated cost-sharing; prioritize behaviour change interventions

4.2.5 Participatory community assessment

Action: Conduct participatory community mapping and assessment

Lead: Committee with technical support from WASH and nutrition specialists

Assessment methods: Participatory mapping, focus group discussions, key informant interviews, household surveys, observation of practices/infrastructure.

Priority assessment areas:

- *Water*: sources, access, quality, management.
- *Sanitation*: facilities, practices, barriers.
- *Hygiene*: knowledge, practices, enabling factors.
- *Nutrition*: status of vulnerable groups, feeding practices, food security, care practices, gender dynamics.

Implementation steps:

1. Train community members as assessment facilitators; develop locally appropriate tools.
2. Ensure inclusive participation across age, gender, and diversity.
3. Analyse findings jointly with community representatives; validate through feedback sessions.
4. Use findings to inform integrated response planning.

4.2.6 Leveraging existing community structures

Action: Map and engage existing community platforms and networks

Lead: Committee with support from community leaders and social mobilizers

Key platforms: Care groups/mother support networks, savings associations, faith-based groups, traditional leadership, youth groups/school committees, water management committees, community health volunteer networks.

Engagement strategies:

- Map existing structures, reach, and influence; identify strategic entry points.
- Engage leaders and influencers for message dissemination; build on existing trust relationships.
- Strengthen the capacity of local networks for sustained engagement.

Implementation steps:

1. Conduct stakeholder and social network analysis.
2. Develop an engagement plan with each key platform; train leaders on integrated WASH/nutrition approaches.
3. Establish a regular information exchange; monitor effectiveness.

4.2.7 Integrated strategy development

Action: Develop joint, multisectoral WASH and nutrition strategies and plans

Lead: Committee with technical advisers from WASH and nutrition sectors

Strategy components:

- Shared objectives and outcomes based on assessment findings.
- Integrated interventions addressing underlying causes of malnutrition.
- Context-specific behaviour change approaches leveraging community assets.
- Harmonized communication messages and delivery channels.
- Costed, multisectoral workplans with clear responsibilities.
- Links to long-term resilience and development goals.

Planning process:

1. Analyse assessment findings to identify priorities; facilitate community-led prioritization.
2. Design integrated activities addressing multiple objectives; identify resources, capacities, and gaps.
3. Develop detailed implementation plans with timelines and community-validated M&E framework.

4.2.8 Communication and feedback mechanisms

Action: Establish two-way communication, referral, and feedback systems

Lead: Committee with support from communication specialists

Communication channels: Focus groups/community dialogues, call-in/community radio, community meetings/information boards, mobile messaging/phone trees, community volunteers/outreach workers.

Referral pathway development:

- Map all WASH, nutrition, and health services; develop clear identification and referral protocols.

- Train volunteers on issue identification; create simple referral forms and tracking systems.
- Establish follow-up mechanisms for referred cases.

Feedback mechanism requirements:

- Multiple accessible channels (verbal, written, technological) with anonymous options.
- Clear procedures and designated focal points for handling feedback.
- Regular analysis of trends; transparency about actions taken.

Implementation: Design contextually appropriate tools; train on feedback handling; raise community awareness; establish a documentation system; report back to the community on actions taken.

4.2.9 School-based integration

Action: Engage schools and educational institutions as integration entry points

Lead: Committee with education partners, school administration, and parent–teacher associations

Key integration opportunities:

- *Infrastructure*: WASH-in-schools, school feeding/nutrition programmes, school gardens.
- *Education*: Student hygiene clubs, peer education, teacher training on integrated WASH/nutrition.
- *Outreach*: Parent education through school platforms and community education sessions.

Implementation steps:

1. Assess existing school WASH and nutrition conditions; develop comprehensive improvement plans.
2. Train teachers and administrators as change agents; establish student clubs and peer programmes.
3. Engage parent–teacher associations in programme design; create links between school and community programmes.

4. Use schools as platforms for community events, demonstrations, and campaigns; train students as household change agents.

4.2.10 Coordination review and adaptation

Action: Establish processes for regular review and adaptation of coordination mechanisms

Lead: Committee with support from WASH and nutrition sector coordination specialists

Review areas: Progress against objectives; effectiveness of coordination structures; quality of information sharing and joint planning; inclusivity and community representation; adaptability to changing context.

Review process:

- Schedule periodic reviews (frequency based on the emergency phase).
- Collect feedback from diverse stakeholders; analyse strengths, weaknesses, and gaps.
- Document lessons learned and good practices; identify improvement opportunities.

Adaptation mechanisms:

- Regular review of committee composition, meeting frequency, and formats.
- Refine communication and information-sharing processes.
- Streamline coordination structures as emergency stabilizes; institutionalize effective practices.

4.2.11 Transition and sustainability

Action: Develop transition and exit strategies from the outset of the emergency response

Lead: Committee with support from development partners and local authorities

Key transition elements:

- Identify and build the capacity of local actors for leadership.

- Progressive shift of decision-making and resource management to community structures.
- Integration of emergency response into long-term development plans.
- Sustainable financing mechanisms for continued activities.

Capacity-building approaches: Skill transfer through mentorship/shadowing, formal training, learning exchanges, documentation of processes, on-the-job coaching.

Implementation steps:

1. Include transition planning in the emergency actions strategy; identify capacity needs.
2. Establish milestones and benchmarks for a progressive transition.
3. Monitor readiness for increasing local responsibility.
4. Document and celebrate achievements; maintain light support structures after formal exit.

4.3 Emergency WASH actions

The emergency WASH actions outlined in this section provide a roadmap for swift, coordinated, and context-specific interventions to address the critical WASH needs of nutritionally vulnerable populations during humanitarian crises. The framework prioritizes life-saving measures in the emergency actions phase (days 0–14), followed by a concerted effort to integrate WASH interventions with local capacity, ensuring sustainable and resilient solutions in the days 14–90 timeframe.

4.3.1 Emergency actions (days 0–14)

The emergency actions phase (days 0–14) is critical for swiftly addressing the most pressing WASH needs and risks faced by nutritionally vulnerable populations in emergencies. Key actions include conducting rapid joint assessments, implementing a minimum WASH package, integrating WASH into community-based nutrition programmes, and collaborating with local actors for harmonized, localized interventions. These foundational steps aim to protect the nutritional status and well-being of affected communities while fostering community engagement and ownership from the outset.

4.3.1.1 Rapidly assess WASH and nutrition at the community level

Timing: Initiate within 72 hours; complete data collection, analysis, and dissemination within 10 days.

Key steps:

1. Engage community leaders, health workers, caregivers, and at-risk group representatives to map water points, sanitation practices, existing WASH infrastructure, and community-based nutrition programmes.
2. Use participatory tools (focus groups, community mapping) alongside standardized methodologies (SMART, WASH KAP, mid-upper arm circumference, infant and young child feeding (IYCF) surveys) to capture needs, priorities, and capacities.
3. Assess household and community-level WASH/nutrition risk factors: disease prevalence, water/sanitation access, hygiene and food-handling practices, environmental cleanliness, and infant/young child feeding behaviours.
4. Analyse findings collaboratively with nutrition, health, and food security actors to identify priority risks, target groups, and integration opportunities.
5. *Days 1–3*: Establish assessment coordination structures; identify local data collection capacity; conduct secondary data review; select locally adapted tools.
6. *Days 3–10*: Mobilize and train gender-balanced, inclusive assessment teams; conduct primary data collection using mixed methods (including remote approaches where needed).

4.3.1.2 Implement minimum WASH package in collaboration with the community

Timing: Roll out within the first 14 days, prioritizing most at-risk communities and groups.

Key steps:

1. *Safe water access*: Rehabilitate damaged water points with community input; distribute treatment kits and storage containers to vulnerable households; promote household water treatment and storage practices.
2. *Sanitation*: Facilitate community-led approaches (community-led total sanitation); install gender-segregated emergency latrines with handwashing and menstrual hygiene management facilities; distribute construction materials; ensure all facilities are inclusive and safe.
3. *Hygiene promotion*: Engage local leaders in behaviour change campaigns; conduct demonstrations at schools and public spaces; co-design inclusive hygiene kits and handwashing stations; use local media and influencers.
4. *Child-safe environment*: Encourage safe child feces disposal; support baby WASH facilities; promote clean play and feeding areas; distribute cleaning kits with caregiver training.
5. *Food safety*: Build caregiver capacity through participatory cooking demonstrations, breastfeeding/complementary feeding promotion, and food hygiene kit distribution with hands-on support.
6. *By day 14*: Launch a locally tailored minimum service package with the community WASH/nutrition coordination committee based on rapid assessment findings, ensuring community ownership.

4.3.1.3 Integrate WASH into community-based nutrition programmes and platforms

Timing: Initiate within the first 14 days; strengthen throughout emergency and recovery phases.

Key steps:

1. *Community health workforce (CHW)*: Train and equip CHWs, nutrition volunteers, and growth-monitoring promoters to deliver integrated WASH/nutrition messages, refer children with WASH-related illnesses, and conduct joint home visits with WASH promoters.

2. *Care groups and nutrition platforms*: Embed hygiene messages into curricula; train model mothers and champions; establish referral systems between nutrition groups and WASH committees; ensure safe water for formula preparation where artificial feeding is supported.
3. *Health and nutrition facilities*: Install/maintain handwashing stations and drinking water points; ensure safe hygiene and food-handling conditions; distribute WASH kits with caregiver education for children with acute malnutrition.
4. *Schools*: Integrate WASH/nutrition content into school activities; train teachers as role models; upgrade facilities to be child friendly and gender sensitive.

4.3.1.4 Collaborate with community actors and authorities for harmonized, localized interventions

Timing: Map stakeholders and convene initial coordination within seven days; continue engagement throughout the response.

Key steps:

1. Establish inclusive, multi-stakeholder WASH/nutrition coordination at subnational and local levels; engage community leaders, the government, civil society, and the private sector in joint planning, implementation, and progress reviews.
2. Develop localized tools, targeting criteria, communication materials, and monitoring systems, reflecting community needs; harmonize messages and service delivery models for consistency and cultural relevance.
3. Mobilize existing community structures (health committees, women's groups, youth clubs, faith-based networks); provide training, resources, and mentoring for outreach, monitoring, and referral activities.
4. Support the establishment or revitalization of community-based WASH infrastructure management systems; build the technical, financial, and organizational capacity of water committees, sanitation groups, and school clubs.
5. *Within seven days*: Map community actors and assets; hold initial coordination meetings to align approaches; regularly update localization strategies based on evolving needs and feedback.

4.3.2 Resilience actions (days 14–90)

Building on the emergency actions efforts, the days 14–90 period focuses on strengthening the integration of emergency WASH interventions with local capacities for long-term resilience and sustainability. Key strategies include assessing and building the technical, organizational, and financial capacities of local WASH and nutrition actors, mobilizing community assets and champions, forging multi-stakeholder partnerships, and planning for a smooth transition to community-managed, risk-informed services.

4.3.2.1 Transition to local leadership and ownership

Timing: Initiate transition planning within the first 30 days; gradually transfer responsibilities throughout the recovery and development phases.

Key steps:

1. Develop a phased transition plan with community representatives, outlining the timeline for handing over WASH infrastructure management, healthy practice promotion, and progress monitoring to local actors.
2. Provide regular on-the-job training, mentoring, and accompaniment to CHWs, WASH committees, school health clubs, and other local structures; use adult learning methods, emphasizing hands-on practice and peer support.
3. Advocate for meaningful community participation in subnational WASH/nutrition coordination platforms, ensuring local priorities inform planning, resource allocation, and policy decisions.
4. Facilitate community-driven sustainable management and financing models (tariff systems, cross-subsidies, collective savings); link to government programmes and long-term funding streams.
5. Conduct participatory capacity self-assessments with key community structures; tailor capacity-building plans to enable increasing local responsibility.

4.3.2.2 Align community-level interventions with national systems

Timing: Review national frameworks and engage stakeholders within the first 30 days; continue harmonization throughout the recovery and development phases.

Key steps:

1. Review national WASH/nutrition policies, strategies, and guidelines; work with government stakeholders to adapt frameworks to the local context while maintaining core standards.
2. Support subnational authorities to contextualize national training curricula, job aids, and behaviour change materials for local languages, customs, and learning needs.
3. Engage community representatives and the local government in multi-stakeholder processes to feed local priorities and lessons into subnational and national policies.
4. Establish clear roles, responsibilities, and coordination mechanisms for local government actors; strengthen institutional capacities and accountability systems.
5. Orient community leaders, WASH committees, and nutrition volunteers on national standards; collaboratively address divergences while respecting community norms.

4.3.2.3 Establish coordination and referral mechanisms between community and facility WASH and nutrition services

Timing: Establish initial protocols within 30 days; continuously strengthen linkages throughout the emergency, recovery, and development phases.

Key steps:

1. Establish context-specific protocols for identifying, referring, and following up WASH-related illnesses; train WASH promoters on the available nutrition services and acute malnutrition identification/referral.
2. Integrate key WASH/nutrition indicators into community-based surveillance, growth monitoring, and health information systems; build frontline worker capacity for integrated data use.

3. Set up accessible community feedback mechanisms (hotlines, SMS reporting); regularly review and act on input with local authorities and service providers.
4. Conduct periodic joint assessments of community and facility-based services to identify bottlenecks and develop collaborative improvement plans; use quality improvement methods to scale effective approaches.
5. Map available WASH/nutrition services; analyse barriers and enablers to coordination; develop practical solutions, leveraging existing resources and systems.

4.3.2.4 Identify and support community-led innovations and adaptations

Timing: Establish participatory innovation processes within the first 45 days; continue to identify, test, and scale promising solutions throughout all phases.

Key steps:

1. Engage community members – particularly women, youth, and marginalized groups – in participatory research and human-centred design to co-create WASH technologies and behaviour change approaches.
2. Document, validate, and build upon indigenous knowledge and practices; leverage positive norms while addressing harmful misconceptions or taboos.
3. Mobilize community champions (elders, religious leaders, traditional healers) to promote key messages and role model positive practices; equip with culturally relevant communication tools.
4. Facilitate peer-to-peer learning, exchange visits, and healthy competition between communities; use community-driven metrics and recognition systems to incentivize achievements.
5. Establish participatory learning and action cycles within community structures; provide flexible seed funding, technical support, and partnership brokering to test and scale promising approaches.

4.3.2.5 Assess and create plans for community-driven WASH and nutrition

Timing: As the situation stabilizes and local capacities grow, conduct in-depth assessments and develop long-term, costed action plans.

Key steps:

1. Work with community WASH/nutrition committees and local authorities to identify information needs, knowledge gaps, and strategic planning priorities; define the scope of in-depth assessments.
2. Build the community capacity to design, lead, and participate in comprehensive assessments, emphasizing data collection skills, ethical practices, and participatory analysis.
3. Facilitate inclusive, community-driven processes to analyse findings, identify root causes, and develop multi-year costed action plans; ensure active participation of women, youth, persons with disabilities, and marginalized groups.
4. Support communities to mobilize internal and external resources; broker partnerships with the government, donors, the private sector, and civil society to address funding and technical gaps.
5. Promote continuous learning and adaptation; embed participatory M&E and knowledge management systems for real-time feedback and evidence-based adjustments.

4.3.2.6 Promote nutrition-sensitive WASH programming

Timing: Integrate nutrition considerations from the early emergency response; strengthen nutrition sensitivity throughout the transition and development phases.

Key steps:

1. Integrate nutrition objectives and indicators into community WASH strategies, prioritizing food hygiene, environmental sanitation, and IYCF practices; engage communities in identifying critical nutrition–WASH linkages.
2. Collaborate with food security, agriculture, and health actors on multisectoral interventions: safe food handling, WASH in

markets/food-processing areas, integration into care groups, and positive deviance/hearth programmes.

3. Strengthen multisectoral coordination platforms; advocate for nutrition-sensitive WASH in local government plans, budgets, and monitoring; establish joint targeting criteria and referral protocols for high-risk households.
4. Integrate nutrition-sensitive WASH messaging into routine health/nutrition services, targeting pregnant/lactating women, caregivers of children under two, and vulnerable groups; train frontline workers to deliver contextual WASH/nutrition counselling.
5. Monitor and evaluate nutrition-sensitive WASH interventions using output, outcome, and impact indicators; conduct joint reviews with nutrition/health stakeholders to assess the WASH contribution to nutrition outcomes.

4.4 Monitoring

4.4.1 Key monitoring activities

4.4.1.1 Engaging communities

Meaningful community involvement throughout the monitoring cycle is essential for relevant, actionable insights. Diverse community members should lead in prioritizing indicators, collecting data, analysing results, and planning improvements.

- Engage community leaders, volunteers, and representatives in designing WASH/nutrition assessments, reflecting local priorities.
- Train and support community-monitoring teams to collect and interpret data using participatory methods.
- Facilitate community-led analysis and validation through accessible formats and inclusive dialogues.
- Establish feedback and accountability systems: community meetings, suggestion boxes/hotlines, social audits, scorecards, citizen report cards.
- Identify and strengthen existing community capacities, positive practices, and indigenous knowledge.

4.4.1.2 Harmonizing indicators and systems

Indicators should be locally relevant while aligning with national and global reporting systems.

- Develop a contextualized WASH/nutrition monitoring framework with core indicators harmonized with national systems.
- Integrate community-level indicators into subnational and national information management systems.
- Harmonize data collection tools, quality controls, and reporting formats across all levels.
- Establish data sharing and coordination mechanisms for joint analysis and use.

4.4.1.3 Strengthening community capacities

Capacity strengthening should emphasize practical application, learning by doing, and participatory approaches.

- Train community monitors on data collection, management, analysis, and use through adult learning methods and on-the-job mentoring.
- Develop simple, visual monitoring tools adapted to local contexts, languages, and literacies.
- Facilitate community-to-community learning exchanges and peer mentoring.
- Advocate for policies and resources to sustain and scale community-led monitoring systems.

4.4.1.4 Utilizing monitoring data

Translating data into action requires user-friendly information, participatory interpretation, and functioning feedback loops.

- Analyse data to assess coverage, quality, and equity of interventions; identify bottlenecks.
- Monitor for unintended consequences: market/service disruption, environmental sustainability issues, protection risks or power imbalances.
- Triangulate with data from health/disease surveillance, food security assessments, school health records, and protection monitoring.

- Produce accessible visual reports, dashboards, and scorecards for different stakeholders.
- Convene participatory spaces for communities, authorities, and partners to review results and plan improvements.
- Use community evidence to advocate for improved policies; collaborate with research institutions to scale successful models.

4.4.2 Key monitoring indicators

Domain	*Indicators*
Nutrition and health status	Stunting, wasting, underweight prevalence (under five); exclusive breastfeeding (0–5 months); minimum acceptable diet (6–23 months); anaemia in pregnant/lactating women and children; diarrhea and WASH-related disease incidence (under five)
WASH practices and services	Safe water handling/storage; basic sanitation access and use; safe child feces disposal; handwashing facilities with soap/water; clean/safe play spaces (under two); caregiver food hygiene practices; schools and health centres with functional WASH facilities
Community mobilization and governance	Functional WASH/nutrition committees and plans; community members trained on integrated promotion; community satisfaction with services and participation in decision-making

4.4.3 Monitoring methods and tools

- *Community-level*: WASH/nutrition mapping, transect walks, participatory observations, scorecards, social audits.
- *Household-level*: Surveys and interviews on practices and coverage; focus group discussions on perceptions, barriers, and priorities.
- *Records review*: Health facility and school records; committee meeting minutes and activity tracking forms.

4.4.4 Monitoring roles and responsibilities

Actor	*Key responsibilities*
Community	Identify/prioritize issues and indicators; collect and compile data; analyse results and develop action plans; share findings with coordination platforms

(*Continues*)

(Continued)

Actor	*Key responsibilities*
Implementing agencies	Co-design participatory monitoring systems; train and coach monitors; provide supportive supervision and quality assurance; facilitate learning and adaptation; synthesize data for sectoral reporting
Government	Coordinate community-based monitoring per national policies; integrate into national systems; convene joint review events; allocate resources; use evidence for policy improvements

4.4.5 Monitoring timeline and deliverables

Frequency	*Activity*
Monthly	Monitoring visits and data collection
Bi-monthly	Community review and action planning meetings
Quarterly	Assessments (emergency phase); data consolidation and submission to subnational platforms
Annual	Participatory evaluations and learning events

Key deliverables:

- Monitoring framework, tools, and training materials.
- Quarterly monitoring reports and scorecards.
- Case studies and learning briefs on monitoring approaches and results.
- Annual reports on system functionality and performance.
- Policy briefs and advocacy materials for institutionalizing community-led monitoring.
- Documentation of innovations and good practices.

ANNEX 1

Quick start guide for emergency actors

This quick start guide links each section of the guide to corresponding resources in the Practitioners' Toolkit, which is published as Annex 1 of the full text.

What's different in this approach?

Key innovations for resource-constrained settings:

Strengths-based assessment: Start by mapping community assets and capacities, not just deficits (full text, section 2.2).

Integrated coordination: Single platform for WASH/health/nutrition instead of separate clusters (full text, section 2.3).

Community leadership: Local actors lead from day 1, not after 'capacity building' (full text, section 2.4).

Flexible programming: Adapt global standards to local realities rather than rigid adherence (full text, Foundational principles for integrated WASH programming).

Sustainable from the start: Build local management into the emergency response, not as an afterthought (full text, section 4.2).

Critical actions for integrated WASH response

Immediate action (hours 0–48)	*Assessment and planning (days 1–14)*
1. **Activate coordination** a. Guidelines 1.2.4, 2.2.4 b. Toolkit 1.1, 1.2 2. **Convene stakeholders** a. Guidelines 1.2.5, 2.2.5, 3.2.5, 4.2.5 b. Toolkit 1.5, 1.6 3. **Establish structures** a. Guidelines 3.2.4, 4.2.4 b. Toolkit 4.8	1. **Conduct assessments** a. Guidelines 1.3.1.1, 2.3.1.1, 3.3.1.1, 4.3.1.1 b. Toolkit 2.1, 2.2, 2.3 2. **Provide emergency services** a. Guidelines 1.3.1.2, 1.3.1.3, 1.3.1.4 b. Guidelines 4.3.1.2 3. **Integrate programmes** a. Guidelines 2.3.1.3 b. Toolkit 4.3, 4.4

Systems establishment (days 14–30)	*Resilience building (days 30–90)*
1. **Set up monitoring** a. All guidelines 1.4, 2.4, 3.4, 4.4 b. Toolkit 5.1, 5.3 2. **Build feedback systems** a. Guidelines 3.2.8, 4.2.8 b. Toolkit 5.3 3. **Develop joint plans** a. Guidelines 1.2.7, 2.2.7 b. Toolkit 3.1, 3.7	1. **Strengthen capacity** a. Guidelines 1.3.2.1, 1.3.2.2, 2.3.2.1, 2.3.2.2, 3.3.2.1, 3.3.2.2, 4.3.2.1, 4.3.2.2 b. Toolkit 3.4, 4.2 2. **Develop sustainability** a. Guidelines 3.3.2.3 b. Guidelines 4.3.2.2 3. **Document learning** a. Guidelines 1.3.2.5, 1.3.2.6, 4.3.2.5, 4.3.2.6 b. Toolkit 5.5

Immediate actions (hours 0–48)

Priority action	*Traditional approach*	*Integrated approach*	*Who leads?*	*Details found in*
1. Activate coordination	• Separate WASH cluster • Separate health cluster • Separate nutrition cluster	• Single integrated platform • Joint WASH/ health/nutrition leadership • Unified decision-making	Government and WASH cluster/health cluster	• Guidelines, 1.2.4, 2.2.4 • Toolkit 1.1, 1.2
2. Convene stakeholders	• Sector-specific meetings • International agency focus	• Multisector meeting • Community leaders as co-chairs • Local actors in leadership roles	Platform co-chairs	• Guidelines 1.2.5, 2.2.5, 3.2.5, 4.2.5 • Toolkit 1.5, 1.6
3. Establish structures	• Top-down task forces • Technical focus only	• Community committees included • Technical and local knowledge • Clear accountability to communities	Local authority and partners	• Guidelines 3.2.4, 4.2.4 • Toolkit 4.8

Assessment and planning (days 1–14)

Priority action	*Traditional approach*	*Integrated approach*	*Who leads?*	*Details found in*
4. Conduct assessments	• Separate sectoral assessments • Focus on gaps/needs • External assessment teams	• Joint WASH/health/nutrition assessment • Map capacities and needs • Community-led data collection	Assessment teams and communities	• Guidelines 1.3.1.1, 2.3.1.1, 3.3.1.1, 4.3.1.1 • Toolkit 2.1, 2.2, 2.3
5. Provide emergency services	• Blanket distributions • Standard packages • Agency-led delivery	• Target vulnerable households • Adapt to local context • Community-managed distribution	WASH sector and communities	• Guidelines 1.3.1.2, 1.3.1.3, 1.3.1.4, 4.3.1.2
6. Integrate programmes	• Parallel service delivery • Missed opportunities	• WASH in all health/nutrition sites • Joint hygiene promotion • Unified messaging	All sectors	• Guidelines 2.3.1.3 • Toolkit 4.3, 4.4

Establishing systems (days 14–30)

Priority action	*Traditional approach*	*Integrated approach*	*Who leads?*	*Details found in*
7. Set up monitoring	• Separate indicators • Agency reporting • Output focus	• Common indicators • Community scorecards • Outcome tracking	M&E teams and communities	• Guidelines 1.4, 2.4, 3.4, 4.4 • Toolkit 5.1, 5.3
8. Build feedback systems	• Complaints boxes • One-way communication	• Multiple channels • Two-way dialogue • Rapid response to feedback	Community committees	• Guidelines 3.2.8, 4.2.8 • Toolkit 5.3
9. Develop joint plans	• Sector-specific plans • Short-term focus	• Integrated action plans • Link emergency to development • Community priorities central	Platform and communities	• Guidelines 1.2.7, 2.2.7 • Toolkit 3.1, 3.7

Building resilience (days 30–90)

Priority action	*Traditional approach*	*Integrated approach*	*Who leads?*	*Details found in*
10. Strengthen capacity	• One-off trainings • Focus on technicians • External trainers	• Continuous mentoring • Whole community approach • Peer-to-peer learning	Local institutions	• Guidelines 1.3.2.1, 1.3.2.2, 2.3.2.1, 2.3.2.2, 3.3.2.1, 3.3.2.2, 4.3.2.1, 4.3.2.2 • Toolkit 3.4, 4.2
11. Develop sustainability	• Plan exit strategy • Handover at end • Donor dependent	• Build from day 1 • Local market solutions • Multiple funding sources	Communities and government	• Guidelines 3.3.2.3, 4.3.2.2
12. Document learning	• External evaluation • Top-down lessons	• Community-led review • Continuous adaptation • Share innovations	All stakeholders	• Guidelines 1.3.2.5, 1.3.2.6, 2.3.2.5, 2.3.2.6, 3.3.2.5, 3.3.2.6, 4.3.2.5, 4.3.2.6 • Toolkit 5.5

Decision support: what to prioritize and when

With minimal resources (must do)

Action	*Target*	*Timeframe*	*Quick reference*
Integrated coordination	All levels	48 hours	Guidelines 1.2.4, 2.2.4, 3.2.4, 4.2.4
Joint assessment	High-risk areas	Days 1–5	Guidelines 1.3.1.1, 2.3.1.1, 3.3.1.1, 4.3.1.1
Safe water (15L/day)	All populations	Days 1–14	Guidelines 1.3.1.2, 2.3.1.2, 3.3.1.2, 4.3.1.2

(*Continues*)

(Continued)

Action	*Target*	*Timeframe*	*Quick reference*
Sanitation near water	Disease hot spots	Days 1–14	Guidelines 1.3.1.3, 2.3.1.3, 3.3.1.3, 4.3.1.2
Handwashing promotion	Vulnerable groups	Days 1–14	Guidelines 1.3.1.4, 3.3.1.3, 4.3.
Community feedback	All sites	By day 14	Guidelines 1.2.8, 2.2.8, 3.2.11, 4.2.11

With moderate resources (should do)

Action	*Target*	*Timeframe*	*Quick reference*
WASH in health facilities	Priority facilities	Days 7–30	Guidelines 1.3.1.6, 3.3.1.2, 3.3.1.5, 4.3.1.2
Nutrition site WASH	All outpatient therapeutic programme/ supplementary feeding programme sites	Days 7–30	Guidelines 2.3.1.3, 4.3.1.3
Local capacity building	WASH committees	Days 14–60	Guidelines 1.3.2.1, 2.3.2.1, 3.3.2.1, 4.3.2.1
Market development	Urban/peri-urban	Days 30–90	Guidelines 3.3.2.2, 4.3.2.2
Integrated monitoring	All programmes	Day 30 onwards	Guidelines 1.4, 2.4, 3.4, 4.4

With adequate resources (could do)

Action	*Target*	*Timeframe*	*Quick reference*
Climate-resilient infrastructure	All systems	Days 30–90	Guidelines 1.3.2.3, 2.3.2.3, 3.3.2.4, 4.3.2.1
Government system strengthening	National/district	Days 30–90	Guidelines 1.2.7, 1.3.2.1, 2.2.10, 2.3.2.1
Policy integration	National level	Days 45–90	Guidelines 1.2.8, 2.2.8
Comprehensive M&E	All interventions	Throughout	Guidelines 1.4, 2.4, 3.4, 4.4

Where to find detailed guidance

If you need to ...	*Refer to:*
Set up coordination mechanisms	Guidelines, sections 1.2 and 2.2; Toolkit sections 1.1–1.7
Conduct integrated assessments	Guidelines, sections 1.3.1.1, 2.3.1.1, 3.3.1.1, and 4.3.1.1; Toolkit sections 2.1–2.6
Plan integrated responses	Guidelines, sections 1.2.7 and 2.2.7; Toolkit sections 3.1–3.7
Implement WASH interventions	Guidelines, sections 1.3, 2.3, 3.3, and 4.4; Toolkit sections 4.1–4.10
Monitor and adapt	Guidelines, sections 1.4, 2.4, 3.4, and 4.4; Toolkit sections 5.1–5.6
Engage communities	Guidelines, sections 3.2 and 4.2; Toolkit section 3.3
Build sustainability	Guidelines, sections 1.3.2, 2.3.2, 3.3.2, and 4.3.2; all case studies throughout the full text

This guide provides entry points to the full guidelines. The five key innovations above (see the Introduction and briefs 1–4) represent the fundamental shifts needed to implement integrated WASH programming successfully in resource-constrained settings.

ANNEX 2

Foundational principles for integrated WASH programming

The following guiding principles translate the understanding of CCP pressures, and the integrated approach outlined in chapter 1 into actionable standards for implementation. These principles apply across all four coordination guidelines and should guide decision-making throughout the emergency response cycle. They represent the essential commitments that underpin effective WASH programming in humanitarian contexts.

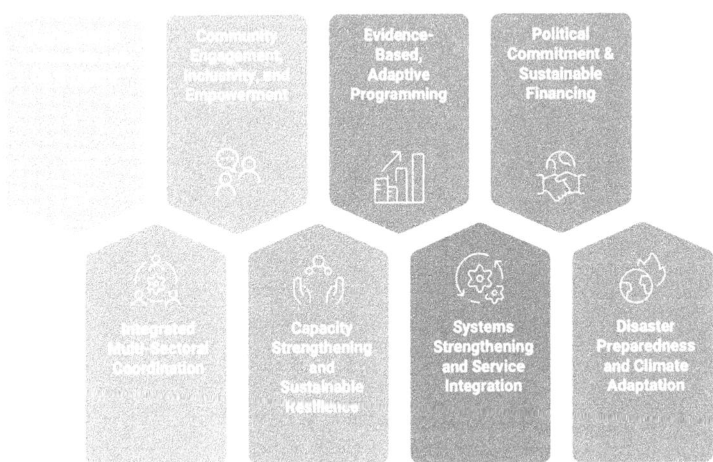

Humanitarian imperative and do no harm

Prioritize life-saving WASH interventions that prevent disease outbreaks, reduce mortality, and address malnutrition while aligning with national humanitarian priorities. Ensure assistance is impartial, reaches the most vulnerable populations (including women, children, elderly people, people with disabilities, and marginalized communities), and promotes dignity without causing unintended harm. Analyse and mitigate potential negative consequences while maintaining clear accountability mechanisms.

Integrated multisectoral coordination

Establish and lead coordination platforms that bring together WASH, health, nutrition, education, food security, and other relevant sectors for collaborative planning and implementation. Adopt a 'health in all policies' approach that systematically addresses social, economic, and environmental determinants. Promote policy coherence, joint planning, and resource optimization while ensuring regular communication and information sharing among all stakeholders at both national and community levels.

Community engagement, inclusivity, and empowerment

Position communities as co-developers and key partners across all aspects of WASH programming, from assessment to implementation and monitoring. Ensure participatory decision-making that actively includes women, youth, people with disabilities, and marginalized groups. Build on existing community structures, knowledge, and coping strategies while establishing accessible feedback mechanisms and promoting social accountability initiatives.

Capacity strengthening and sustainable resilience

Strengthen institutional capacity at all levels through ongoing mentorship, peer learning, and systems strengthening beyond one-off training. Partner with local actors to build technical, managerial, and institutional capacity for sustainable service delivery. Design climate-resilient WASH systems and invest in emergency preparedness while progressively shifting ownership and decision-making to local structures.

Evidence-based, adaptive programming

Establish robust systems for collecting, analysing, and using disaggregated data to guide decision-making and enable adaptive management. Develop context-specific strategies that adapt global standards (including Sphere standards) to local realities. Create participatory monitoring systems that track integrated outcomes across sectors and foster continuous learning and improvement.

Systems strengthening and service integration

Implement WASH interventions within broader health and nutrition systems strengthening frameworks. Ensure WASH activities align with public health priorities, surveillance systems, and nutrition objectives. Focus on comprehensive packages of interventions that address multiple determinants of health and well-being, using simple, low-cost solutions that leverage existing resources.

Political commitment and sustainable financing

Secure high-level political commitment for integrated WASH programming across government ministries and donor agencies. Advocate for prioritization of WASH in health, nutrition, and development policies, strategies, and budgets. Establish clear institutional roles, responsibilities, and accountability mechanisms while mobilizing resources for infrastructure, services, and personnel at all levels.

Disaster preparedness and climate adaptation

Integrate disaster risk reduction, emergency preparedness, and climate resilience into all WASH planning and implementation. Develop multi-hazard contingency plans, strengthen early warning systems, and promote climate-adaptive technologies. Build local capacity to anticipate, mitigate, and respond to future shocks while maintaining agile coordination mechanisms that can adapt to evolving needs.

ANNEX 3

Sources consulted in the creation of the guidelines

These guidelines were created with the generous help of WASH, health, and nutrition professionals from various government, NGO, and UN organizations. In addition to their input, the following sources were also referenced in the creation of these guidelines.

Action Against Hunger (ACF). 2015. 'Link NCA Guidelines: A Participatory and Response Oriented Method for Conducting a Nutrition Causal Analysis'. https://linknca.org/methode.htm

Action Against Hunger (ACF). 2017a. 'A Practical Package for Stunting Reduction: Contribution to Malnutrition Reduction Through a Multi-Sector Approach'. https://accioncontraelhambre.org/sites/default/files/documents/2017_babywash_en_0.pdf

Action Against Hunger (ACF). 2017b. *WASH Nutrition: A Practical Guidebook on Increasing Nutritional Impact through Integration of WASH and Nutrition Programmes*. Paris: Action Against Hunger.

Action Against Hunger (ACF) and SMART. 2014. 'Guidelines: Rapid SMART Surveys for Emergencies'. https://smartmethodology.org/survey-planning-tools/smart-methodology/rapid-smart-methodology/

CHS Alliance. 2020. 'PSEAH Implementation Quick Reference Handbook'. https://www.chsalliance.org/get-support/resource/pseah-implementation-quick-reference-handbook/

FHI 360. 2024. *IYCF-E Assessment Guide*. Durham (NC): FHI 360. https://www.nutritioncluster.net/sites/nutritioncluster.com/files/2024-12/IYCF-E-Assessment-Guide-v6.pdf

Global WASH Cluster. 2023. 'Competency Framework for Cluster Coordination'. https://www.washcluster.net/file-download/download/public/52856

Global WASH Cluster. 2024. 'Coordination Resources'. https://www.washcluster.net/coordination-resources

Global WASH Cluster. n.d. 'GWC Coordination Tool Kit (CTK) – Confluence'. https://washcluster.atlassian.net/wiki/spaces/CTK/overview

Institute for Healthcare Improvement. 2017. 'Quality Improvement Essentials Toolkit'. https://www.ihi.org/resources/tools/quality-improvement-essentials-toolkit

Interagency Standing Committee (IASC). 2015. 'Multi-Sector Initial Rapid Assessment (MIRA) Tool'. https://interagencystandingcommittee.org/sites/default/files/migrated/2019-02/mira_manual_2015.pdf

International Federation of Red Cross and Red Crescent Societies. 2017. *WASH Guidelines for Hygiene Promotion in Emergency Operations*. Geneva: International Federation of Red Cross and Red Crescent Societies.

International Federation of Red Cross and Red Crescent Societies. 2021. 'Community Engagement and Accountability (CEA) Toolkit | IFRC'. August 16. https://www.ifrc.org/document/cea-toolkit

Lopez, Jason, Sergio Tumax Sierra, Ana María Rodas Cardona, and Stephen Sara. 2020. 'Implementing the Clean Clinic Approach Improves Water, Sanitation, and Hygiene Quality in Health Facilities in the Western Highlands of Guatemala'. *Global Health: Science and Practice* 8 (2): 256–69. https://doi.org/10.9745/GHSP-D-19-00413

Médecins Sans Frontières. 2018. 'Management of a Cholera Epidemic: Practical Guide for Doctors, Nurses, Laboratory Technicians, Medical Auxiliaries, Water and Sanitation Specialists and Logisticians'. https://medicalguidelines.msf.org/en/viewport/CHOL/english/management-of-a-cholera-epidemic-23444438.html?language_content_entity=en

OECD. 2018. *Implementing the OECD Principles on Water Governance: Indicator Framework and Evolving Practices*. Paris: OECD Publishing. https://doi.org/10.1787/9789264292659-en

Oxfam. 2013. 'A Quick Guide to Monitoring, Evaluation, Accountability and Learning in Fragile Contexts'. https://policy-practice.oxfam.org/resources/a-quick-guide-to-monitoring-evaluation-accountability-and-learning-in-fragile-c-297134/

Oxfam. 2016. 'Guide to Community Engagement in WaSH: A Practitioners' Guide, Based on Lessons from Ebola'. https://policy-practice.oxfam.org/resources/guide-to-community-engagement-in-wash-a-practitioners-guide-based-on-lessons-fr-620139/

SIWI and UNICEF. 2020. *WASH Accountability in Fragile Contexts*. Stockholm and New York: UNICEF-UNDP-SIWI Accountability for Sustainability Partnership. http://www.watergovernance.org/

SMART. 2017. 'Measuring Mortality, Nutritional Status, and Food Security in Crisis Situations: SMART Methodology'. https://smart-methodology.org/survey-planning-tools/smart-methodology/

Sphere Association. 2018. *The Sphere Handbook: Humanitarian Charter and Minimum Standards in Humanitarian Response*, 4th edn. Geneva, Switzerland: Sphere Association. www.spherestandards.org/handbook

UNHCR. 2019. 'Uganda - WASH KAP Survey Palabek Settlement (Refugees & Host Community), October 2019'. https://microdata.unhcr.org/index.php/catalog/253/study-description

UNHCR. 2020. *UNHCR WASH Manual: Practical Guidance for Refugee Settings*. Geneva: UNHCR. https://www.unhcr.org/us/media/unhcr-wash-practical-guidance-refugee-settings

UNICEF. 2013. 'UNICEF Cholera Toolkit'. https://www.washcluster.net/node/29581

UNICEF. 2016. 'Nutrition-WASH Toolkits: Guide for Practical Joint Actions Nutrition-Water, Sanitation and Hygiene (WASH)'. https://www.unicef.org/eap/reports/nutrition-wash-toolkit-guide-practical-joint-actions

UNICEF. 2017. *Sustainability Checks: Guidance to Design and Implement Sustainability Monitoring in WASH*. New York and Stockholm: UNICEF and UNDP-SIWI.

UNICEF. n.d. 'Water, Sanitation and Hygiene'. UNHCR US. https://www.unhcr.org/us/what-we-do/respond-emergencies/water-sanitation-and-hygiene

UNICEF and GWP. 2022. 'Strategic Framework for WASH Climate Resilient Development'. United Nations Children's Fund (UNICEF) and Global Water Partnership (GWP).

UNICEF and SIWI. 2023. *WASH Bottleneck Analysis Tool: Country Implementation Guide*. New York: United Nations Children's Fund (UNICEF).

WASH in Health Care Facilities. n.d. 'WASH in HCF Evaluation and Reporting Tools'. https://washinhcf.org/resource/wash-in-hcf-evaluation-and-reporting tools/

WHO. 2018. *Guidelines on Sanitation and Health*. Geneva: World Health Organization. https://www.who.int/publications/i/item/9789241514705

WHO. 2020. *Health Cluster Guide: A Practical Handbook*. Geneva: World Health Organization. https://healthcluster.who.int/publications/i/item/9789240004726

WHO. 2021. *Strengthening Infection Prevention and Control in Primary Care: A Collection of Existing Standards, Measurement and Implementation Resources*. Geneva: World Health Organization.

WHO. n.d. 'Outbreak Toolkit: Providing the Tools to Investigate Disease Outbreaks, Collect Data and Guide Response Activities'. https://www.who.int/emergencies/outbreak-toolkit

WHO and UNICEF. 2018. 'Core Questions on Drinking Water, Sanitation and Hygiene for Household Surveys: 2018 Update'. United Nations Children's Fund and World Health Organization.

WHO and UNICEF. 2020. *Operational Framework for Primary Health Care: Transforming Vision into Action*. Geneva: World Health Organization and the United Nations Children's Fund.

WHO and UNICEF. 2022. *Water and Sanitation for Health Facility Improvement Tool (WASH FIT): A Practical Guide for Improving Quality of Care through Water, Sanitation and Hygiene in Health Care Facilities*, 2nd edn. Geneva: World Health Organization.

Index

www.ingramcontent.com/pod-product-compliance
Lightning Source LLC
LaVergne TN
LVHW021155160826
845679LV00024B/2138

* 9 7 8 1 7 8 8 5 3 4 7 2 7 *